Conquerors of the Roman Empire: The Vandals

Conquerors of the Roman Empire: The Vandals

Simon MacDowall

Pen & Sword
MILITARY

First published in Great Britain in 2016 by
Pen & Sword Military
An imprint of
Pen & Sword Books Ltd
47 Church Street
Barnsley
South Yorkshire
S70 2AS

ISBN 978 1 47383 770 6

A CIP catalogue record for this book is
available from the British Library

Typeset in Ehrhardt by
Replika Press Pvt Ltd, India
Printed and bound in England
By CPI Group (UK) Ltd, Croydon, CR0 4YY

Pen & Sword Books Ltd incorporates the Imprints of Pen & Sword
Aviation, Pen & Sword Family History, Pen & Sword Maritime, Pen &
Sword Military, Pen & Sword Discovery, Pen & Sword Politics, Pen &
Sword Atlas, Pen & Sword Archaeology, Wharncliffe Local History,
Wharncliffe True Crime, Wharncliffe Transport, Pen & Sword Select, Pen
& Sword Military Classics, Leo Cooper, The Praetorian Press, Claymore
Press, Remember When, Seaforth Publishing and Frontline Publishing.

For a complete list of Pen & Sword titles please contact
PEN & SWORD BOOKS LIMITED
47 Church Street, Barnsley, South Yorkshire, S70 2AS, England
E-mail: enquiries@pen-and-sword.co.uk
Website: www.pen-and-sword.co.uk

Contents

List of Plates

1. A rare depiction of a mounted Germanic warrior. (Landesmuseum für Vorgeschichte, Halle)
2. Silver spurs from a third century Germanic noble's grave. (British Museum, author's photo)
3. Sarmatian warriors depicted on Trajan's Column. (Author's photo)
4. Roman cavalry helmet. (Rijksmuseum voor Oudheden, Leiden, photo Michiel)
5. Page from a medieval copy of the *Notitia Dignitatum* showing the cities under the control of the *Dux Mogontiacensis*. (Bodleian manuscript)
6. A reconstructed ship of the Roman Rhine fleet. (The Museum of Ancient Shipping, Mainz)
7. General Stilicho, his wife Serena and son Eucherius. (Monza Cathedral)
8. Alan wearing scale armour and carrying a lance. (Hermitage Museum, St Petersburg)
9. Fishing boat of a type commandeered by the Vandals. (Bardo Museum, author's photo)
10. Transports for cavalry horses. (Bardo Museum, author's photo)
11. The Dominus Julius' villa in Africa Proconsularis. (Bardo Museum, author's photo)
12. Luxury ceramics known as African *sigillata*. (Bardo Museum, author's photo)
13. North African merchant ship. (Bardo Museum, author's photo)
14. Roman soldiers defending a city from marauding tribesmen. (Museum für Byzantinische Kunst, Berlin)
15. Frontispiece from the *Notitia Dignitatum*. (Bodleian manuscript)
16. Silver plate celebrating the appointment of Flavius Ardabur Aspar as Consul of Africa. (National Archaeological Museum, Florence, photo by Sailko)
17. The ruins of Roman Carthage. (Author's photo)

List of Maps

Chapter 1

Germania

The Vandals

The very name conjures up violent images of wanton destruction. It is the label given to those that deliberately destroy or damage property and it is the lasting epithet of the ancient Germanic tribe that carved a kingdom out of Roman Africa in the fifth century AD.

Of all the conquerors of the Roman Empire the Vandals surely have had the worst press. The Greeks and Romans called anyone living beyond the bounds of their Mediterranean civilization a 'barbarian'. This pejorative term has also found its way into modern usage implying, as it did in ancient times, someone who is uncouth, uneducated and uncivilized. A 'vandal' seems to be one step further beyond the pale.

Who then were these people whose name has been preserved for nearly 1,700 years as the epitome of barbaric savagery? Do they deserve their reputation or is there more to their story?

The original Vandals sacked Rome in 455 but they were not the first to do so. Alaric's Goths captured the eternal city forty years earlier, spending three days looting, pillaging and plundering. St Augustine was living in Hippo Regius as the Vandals were besieging that city, which they later sacked. For many early Christians the horrors of barbarian invasion was seen as God's righteous wrath and punishment for their sins. The Vandals, although Christians themselves by this time, followed the teachings of the Bishop Arius and vigorously persecuted the Romans who believed that the Arian version of Christianity was heresy. All of this added up to an impression that the Vandals were bent on the destruction of all that was good and civilized.

As far as it is possible to tell, the term 'vandalism' first came to be equated with wanton destruction in the eighteenth century. In 1794, Henri Grégoire, the bishop of Blois, described the destruction of artwork in the French Revolution as '*vandalisme*'. The term stuck, even if the original Vandals were perhaps no more or less destructive than any of the other conquerors of ancient Rome. The Vandals are credited with defacing Roman monuments but in truth, much of the destruction of classical architecture was carried out by local inhabitants re-using building materials along with pious Christians taking offence at nudity and pagan symbolism.

Despite the real horrors of invasion by a foreign people who then become unsympathetic overlords, there is indeed much more to the narrative of the Vandals. Their story is actually quite remarkable. After very little contact with the Greco-Roman world, they emerged from the forests of central Europe in the early fifth century. They crossed the Rhine in midwinter, ravaged Gaul (modern France and Belgium) then passed through the Pyrenees. They briefly ruled over parts of Spain but in 429 they were on the move again. They crossed from Spain into Africa and took the Roman province for themselves.

It may be that the name of the Vandals comes from the same root as the modern German '*wandeln*' (in German the letter 'w' is pronounced as the English 'v'). From this we get the English word 'wanderer'. If so it is an apt name. The Vandals were indeed wanderers, moving from Scandinavia to central Europe, then down to the Danube before crossing the Rhine, passing through France into Spain, and finally ending up in Africa.

Once established in Africa, these people from the land-locked forests of central Europe ruled the Mediterranean with their fleets, defying both the West and East Roman Empires. From a small insignificant tribe amongst many, they had emerged as one of the most powerful kingdoms of the fifth century. Their moment in the African sun was, however, very short lived. In 533 the East Romans, under the inspired leadership of Belisarius, crushed the Vandals and wiped out all traces of their kingdom except for the memory of their name as destroyers of civilization.

This book will examine how the Vandals managed to achieve such stunning success and then lose it all in a brief campaign. It will focus on the military aspects: how their armies were formed, their tactics, equipment and how they compared with their opponents. As a consequence the book will concentrate primarily on the great migration that led to the foundation of their African kingdom and its reconquest by Justinian's

East Romans. All of this will be placed in the political, religious and social context of the times.

Our Sources

The Vandals left very little archeological record. Therefore in reconstructing their story we have to rely primarily on literary sources. Unfortunately, unlike many of the other conquerors of the Roman Empire such as the Goths, Franks, Lombards and Saxons, the Vandals had no one to write their history from their point of view. The only contemporary records that we have, were written by their Roman enemies.

The end of the Vandal kingdom is very well documented by Procopius, secretary to the Roman general Belisarius who led the campaign which defeated the Vandals. Procopius was actually present at many of the incidents he recounted and took an active part in the campaign. As a result we have detailed accounts of the battles and skirmishes that took place between the Roman invasion of Africa in 533 and the end of the last free Vandals in 546. Although obviously biased, Procopius's history is reasonably balanced. His descriptions of the battles, the numbers of troops involved and the various political machinations are both realistic and reliable.

The same cannot be said about any of the sources prior to this. Before their crossing of the Rhine in the early-fifth century, the Vandals were a relatively minor Germanic people and are only mentioned in passing by various Roman authors. Once they moved into Roman territory their story is recounted in horror by several chroniclers, all of whom were churchmen who took great exception to the Vandals' heretical beliefs.

After crossing the Rhine on the last day of 406, the Vandals spent three years ravaging France. Yet the sum total of what contemporary chroniclers have to say about this amounts to no more than a few hundred words. Other than listing the cities that fell to the Vandals and some hints of other actions, Saint Jerome, Prosper of Aquitaine and others do not tell us how they did it, what sort of defence the Romans conducted nor any detail of the many skirmishes, sieges and battles that must have taken place between 406 and 409.

Once the Vandals crossed into Spain, the Spanish Bishop Hydatius gives us a little more detail. Hydatius lived through the Vandal occupation of Spain and spent several months as a prisoner of the Suevi who had accompanied the Vandals from Germany into Spain. Even though Hydatius tells us something about the events that took place in his country between 409 and 429, he is terribly short on detail. For example he says: 'the barbarians ran wild through the Spanish provinces', but does not say anything about how they managed to take most of the peninsular for themselves.

The story of the Vandals' early years in Africa suffers from the same problem. Several bishops, Victor of Vita being the most notable, wrote about the suffering of Roman orthodox Christians at the hands of the Vandals. We hear how the Vandals 'set to work on (Africa) with their wicked forces, laying it waste by devastation and bringing everything to ruin with fire and murders.' Once again we do not learn how they did it, nor how they managed to defeat the Roman armies sent against them.

Therefore, in telling the Vandals' fascinating story, I have had to frequently fall back on conjecture. I have tried to piece together the frustratingly sparse contemporary evidence, match it with other original sources that tell us something about the politics and military actions of the age and come up with conclusions that seem right, even if we are unlikely to ever know for certain. In this regard there are a couple of other invaluable contemporary sources. The first of these is the history of Ammianus Marcellinus – a fourth century Roman officer turned historian. Although his history ends a couple of decades before the Vandals crossed the Rhine, he does give first hand accounts of late Roman and barbarian warfare as well as observations on many of the peoples who played into the Vandal story. The second is the *Notitia Dignitatum*, a list of offices and army units from the end of fourth and early-fifth centuries. This tells us the official orders of battle of the Roman Army at the time of the Vandal invasion. While it needs to be treated with a fair degree of caution it is invaluable in building a picture of the Roman Army at the time of the Vandals. The histories and letters of Zosimus, Priscus, Saint Augustine, Olympiodorus, Jordanes, Sidonius Apollinaris and other chroniclers help to fill in some of the blanks.

I have quite deliberately relied on contemporary accounts rather than more recent histories or interpretations. In fact there are very few modern accounts of the Vandal story. The definitive modern study of the Vandals was written by Christian Courtois in 1955 and since then there have only been a couple of new books about them. There have, of course, been many new investigations of the fall of the West Roman Empire and late Roman warfare. Many of these have been very helpful in placing the story of the Vandals in a wider political, military and economic context. I have listed the most useful ones in the bibliography.

The Origins of the Vandals

The Vandals were an east Germanic people who crossed the Rhine in the early fifth century and ended up in Africa. This much is certain. Tracing back their origins and forming any idea of what their ancestors were like is much less so.

Tacitus, in his first century work *Germania*, recounts oral German tradition in which three groups of tribes – the Ingaevones; the Hermiones and the Istaevones were descended from the son of the earth-born god Tuisto. He then goes on to say:

> 'Some authorities, with the freedom of conjecture permitted by remote antiquity, assert that Tuisto had more numerous descendants and mention more tribal groups such as Marsi, Gambrivii, Suevi and Vandillii – names which they affirm to be both genuine and ancient.'

It would seem that Tacitus is sceptical of this claim, even though he is quite tactful in the way he expresses his doubt. Unfortunately, after this brief introduction, Tactius does not mention the Vandals again. When he goes through his descriptions of each of the Germanic tribes he says nothing about the Vandals or Vandillii.

Pliny the Elder also mentions the Vandilii in his *Natural History*, written in AD 77. He lists them as one of the five most important German tribes alongside the Burgundians, Goths, Varini and Charini. Interestingly, Pliny adds that the Burgundians were a part of the Vandal people. Close cooperation between the later Siling Vandals and Burgundians may lend some credence to this claim.

Norse and Germanic legends recount stories of migrations from Scandinavia into central Europe in which the Germanic peoples displaced or absorbed the earlier Celtic inhabitants. This is certainly the Gothic tradition and it is backed up with some archeological and etymological evidence. The same may be true of the Vandals. However, Tacitus' story and Jordanes, history of the Goths may indicate that the Vandals were already living in central Europe when the Goths and others moved south.

Jordanes wrote in the sixth century for a Gothic audience. As such he glorifies the deeds of that people at the expense of others. In the fifth century the Goths and Vandals were bitter enemies. Jordanes traces this enmity back in the mists of time when the Goths first moved from Scandinavia to Germany, 'subdued their neighbours, the Vandals, and thus added to their victories.' By the third century the Goths were settled north of the Black Sea 'holding undisputed sway over great stretches of country, many arms of the sea and many river courses. By their strong right arm the Vandals were often laid low.'

We have to take Jordanes' stories with a grain of salt. A bit like Geoffrey of Monmouth rewriting Arthurian legends for the benefit of King Stephen, he re-interprets ancient histories for his Gothic readers to give them legitimacy. The Vandals are always cast in a bad light while the deeds of the Goths are glorified.

The seventh century *Origin of the Lombard People* recounts a legend in which the Lombards also defeated the Vandals early in their history:

'There is an island that is called Scadanan… where many people dwell. Among these there was a small people that was called the Vinniles. And with them was a woman, Gambara by name, and she had two sons. Ybor and Agio. They, with their mother, Gambara, held the sovereignty over the Vinniles.

'Then the leaders of the Vandals, that is, Ambri and Assi, moved with their army, and said to the Vinniles: "Either pay us tribute or prepare yourselves for battle and fight with us."

'Then answered Ybor and Agio, with their mother Gambara: "It is better for us to make ready the battle than to pay tributes to the Vandals."

'Then Ambri and Assi, that is, the leaders of the Vandals, asked Wodan that he should give them the victory over the Vinniles. Wodan answered, saying: "Whom I shall first see at sunrise, to them will I give the victory."

'At that time Gambara with her two sons... appealed to Frea, the wife of Wodan, to help the Vinniles. Frea gave counsel that at sunrise the Vinniles should come, and that their women, with their hair let down around the face in the likeness of a beard, should also come with their husbands. Then when it became bright, while the sun was rising, Frea, the wife of Wodan, turned around the bed where her husband was lying and put his face towards the east and awakened him. And he, looking at them, saw the Vinniles and their women having their hair let down around their faces. And he says, "Who are these Long-beards?" And Frea said to Wodan, "As you have given them a name, give them also the victory." And he gave them the victory, so that they should defend themselves according to his counsel and obtain the victory. From that time the Vinniles were called Langobards (long-beards).'

It is possible that the Vandals were previous migrants who had to defend their territories from new arrivals such as the Goths and Lombards, although the Lombard history places their conflict with the Vandals in Scandinavia. There are links with the Vandal name to Scandinavia. Vendel in Sweden, called *Vaendil* in old Swedish, may indicate an original homeland of the Vandals. The northern tip of the Jutland peninsular of Denmark is called Vendsyssel, which may also have a Vandal connection. 'Syssel' is an ancient administrative area similar to the English 'shire', and ancient Danish names for the area include *Wendila* and *Wændil*. The ancestors of the Vandals may have migrated from northern Denmark in the second century BC. The archeological record shows that the Jutland peninsular was heavily settled at that time and then shortly afterwards was largely abandoned.

It is probable that the ancestors of the Vandals were living in modern Silesia, which is now part of Poland, at the time that Tacitus wrote his *Germania*. The archeological record shows a common culture over a wide but sparsely-populated area of small settlements where the dead were mostly cremated but notable warriors were interred together with horse gear and spurs.

Unfortunately the links between the literary and archeological records for the early Vandals are tenuous at best. After the brief mention of the Vandals in his introduction, Tacitus says that a confederation of tribes called the Lugi were living in the region where the Vandals are presumed to have settled. The Lugi are also located by other Greek and Roman writers as settled between the Oder and Vistula rivers but their name drops out of the historical record by the second century as that of the Vandals comes into greater prominence. Some historians have concluded that the Lugi and Vandals were one and the same, others think that the Vandals may have absorbed the Lugi in the second century and still others believe that there is no link at all. We will never really know for certain.

Ancient Germanic tribes were not like modern nation-states nor were they necessarily people who shared a common ancestry and heritage. The Vandals who moved into Africa in the fifth century included Alans, a Sarmatian people, and many others who were not descended from the original Vandals of central Europe. Ethnicity amongst the ancient German tribes was more about shared attitudes than ancestry or race. You were a Vandal if you were bound by oaths of loyalty to a Vandal leader and followed the norms and customs of Vandal society. Therefore the early Vandals could be thought of as a constantly shifting community, with various groups joining and leaving over the centuries before the crossing into Africa. This makes tracing their early history a very difficult proposition indeed.

First Contact with Rome

By the second century the story of the Vandals starts to become a little clearer. There are two main groupings: the Asdings (also variously written as Hasdings or Astings) and the Silings. The Silings continued to live in the area between the Oder and Vistula, possibly lending their name to modern Silesia. The Asdings, meanwhile, moved further south into modern Bohemia eventually settling in the Tisza Valley just north of the Roman Danube frontier. It may be that Asding expansion, up against the territories of the Marcomanni and Quadi, was one of the causes that sparked off the Marcomannic wars with Rome (AD 166-180). These were the pre-cursors to the great barbarian migrations of the fourth and fifth centuries. Although the Romans defeated the invaders, the fragility of the Imperial frontier was laid bare. The pattern of tribes beyond Rome's borders being displaced by the aggressive movements of others, then spilling over the Imperial frontier, would be repeated many times in the years that followed.

Other than exerting pressure on the tribes living along the Danube frontier, the role of the Vandals in the Marcomannic wars is not entirely clear. Some Roman sources have the Vandals as allies of the Emperor Marcus Aurelius, while another says that they were defeated by him. Cassius Dio, who is one of the historians who asserts that the Asding Vandals were Roman allies, also tells of a further expansion into Dacia (modern Romania):

'The Astingi, led by their chieftains Raus and Raptus, came into Dacia with their entire households, hoping to secure both money and land in return for their alliance. But failing of their purpose, they left their wives and children under the protection of Clemens [Sextus Cornelius Clemens, Governor of Dacia], until they should acquire the land of the Costoboci by their arms; but upon conquering that people, they proceeded to injure Dacia no less than before. The Lacringi, fearing that Clemens in his dread of them might lead these newcomers into the land which they themselves were inhabiting, attacked them while off their guard and won a decisive victory. As a result, the Astingi committed no further acts of hostility against the Romans, but in response to urgent supplications addressed to Marcus [Aurelius] they received from him both money and the privilege of asking for land in case they should inflict some injury upon those who were then fighting against him. Now this tribe really did fulfil some of its promises.'

The Asding Vandals seem to have profited from the Marcomannic wars. In the peace settlement that followed, they were placed under Roman protection, the Marcomanni were forbidden to make war on them and their newly-won territories along the Dacian border were confirmed. Despite this, another source tells us that the Romans played the Vandals and Marcomanni off against each other in order to weaken them both. At this time the Vandals were still bit players in the drama that was unfolding beyond the Roman frontier. The Sarmatians, Goths, Alamanni, Franks, Suevi Marcomanni and Quadi were the leading actors

Over the next century the historical record goes quiet. Presumably the Vandals settled down for a while. Although they no doubt fought minor actions agains their Germanic and Sarmatian neighbours, relations with Rome remained distant and peaceful. In the mid-third century a series of Gothic invasions devastated the Balkans. The Goths sacked Athens and raided throughout the Aegean. In 248 some Asding Vandals joined the Goths for a raid into Moesia but other than that they seemed to have stayed out of the bitter conflict that followed.

In 270, after the defeat of the Goths at the Battle of Naissus, two Vandal kings apparently joined up with some Sarmatians to invade Pannonia. It is not clear why they chose this moment to invade rather than striking while the Romans were still engaged with the Goths. A plague had just broken out and the Emperor Claudius Gothicus died of it. Perhaps the Vandals and Sarmatians decided to take advantage of the Emperor's death or perhaps they were set on the move by devastation caused by the plague.

It is likely that the Vandals were the junior partners in this expedition as Sarmatians feature most prominently in the original sources. The Vandals, or *Vandeloi* as he calls them, are only mentioned by Publius Herennius Dexippus, a contemporary Athenian historian whose reliability is questionable. The Sarmatians and Vandals were defeated by the new Emperor Aurelian, who took the title of 'Sarmaticus' after his victory. This confirms that the Sarmatians were the main antagonists. Aurelian held a triumph in 274 and Vandal prisoners were apparently paraded before the Roman populace. The defeated barbarians also had to provide 2,000 horsemen to serve in the Roman Army as part of the peace settlement. It is possible that some of these may have been Vandals, although it is highly unlikely that any Vandal band at that time could muster so many warriors. Most probably the vast majority of these men would have been Sarmatians.

At this point in their history the Vandals were still a conglomeration of relatively minor clans rather than a strong cohesive grouping. Bands of them seemed to have operated more or less independently of each other and there was no sense of a Vandal nation beyond the Rhine and Danube frontiers. While bands of Asdings were cooperating with the Sarmatians or fighting their neighbours in the Tisza Valley beyond the Danube, the Silings were pushing up against the Rhine. In the 270s the Emperor Probus defended the Rhine-Danube frontier against a combined force of Siling Vandals and Burgundians. In an engagement on the Lech River in modern Bavaria, Probus is said to have defeated the more numerous Germans by luring them over the river.

'He (Probus) made war on the Burgundi and the Vandili. But seeing that his forces were too weak, he endeavoured to separate those of his enemies, and engage only with part of them. His design was favoured by fortune; for the armies lying on both sides of the river, the Romans challenged the Barbarians that were on the further side to fight. This so incensed them, that many of them crossed over, and fought until the Barbarians were all either slain or taken by the Romans; except a few that remained behind, who sued for peace, on condition of giving up their captives and plunder; which was acceded to. But as they did not restore all that they had taken, the Emperor was so enraged, that he fell on them as they were retiring, killed many of them, and took prisoner their general Igillus. All of them that were taken alive were sent to Britain, where they settled, and were subsequently very serviceable to the Emperor when any insurrection broke out.' (Zosimus)

For the most part of the third and fourth centuries the Vandals were not at war with Rome. Instead their conflicts were primarily with their Sarmatian and Germanic neighbours. A panegyric to the Emperor Maximian in the late third century tells of a victory by the Tervingi and Taifali over the Vandals and Gepids. No doubt there were many similar unrecorded wars as the relatively weak and independent Vandal groups tried to hold onto their lands in face of expansion by their stronger and more cohesive neighbours.

Jordanes gives a detailed account of a war between the Goths and Vandals during the reign of Constantine (306–337):

'Geberich (a Gothic king) ... sought to enlarge his country's narrow bounds at the expense of the race of the Vandals and Visimar, their king. This Visimar was of the stock of the Asdingi, which is eminent among them and indicates a most warlike descent ... The battle raged for a little while on equal terms [by the Maros River in Modern Hungary]. But soon Visimar himself, the King of the Vandals, was overthrown, together with the greater part of his people. When Geberich, the famous leader of the Goths, had conquered and spoiled the Vandals, he returned to his own place whence he had come. Then the remnant of the Vandals who had escaped, collecting a band of their unwarlike folk, left their ill-fated country and asked the Emperor Constantine for Pannonia. Here they made their home for about sixty years and obeyed the commands of the emperors like subjects.'

This is one of the most detailed and seemingly definitive stories we have of early Vandal history by an ancient writer. However, Jordanes wrote his history 200 years after the events he is recounting and he was doing so with hindsight of the Gothic-Vandal enmity of the fifth century. If Constantine had given the Vandals land in Pannonia it would be reasonable to assume that there would be some Roman record of this. Unfortunately there is none, nor is there any mention of this settlement in any other sources, nor archaeological evidence to support it. Quite probably this is an apocryphal story, which may give some indication of the ongoing conflicts between the Vandals and their neighbours rather than fact. Maybe there was a Vandal leader called Visimar, maybe he did fight the Goths and was defeated by them, but it is less likely that any Vandals were given Roman land to settle by Constantine.

Vandals in the Roman Army

For the most part of the second to the fourth centuries the Vandals were a relatively weak conglomeration of groups living beyond the Roman frontiers. Occasionally bands of them fought against Rome and sometimes others were allies. They did not feature prominently in Roman histories and there was no indication that they would become such formidable foes in the future. It is easy to assume that if anyone in the fourth century predicted that these people would soon overrun France, Spain and Africa, they would have been dismissed out of hand.

If the Goths, Sarmatians and Alamanni were the main barbarian threats to the Roman Empire in the third-fourth centuries, the Vandals were seen as a source of likely recruits for the army – the most famous being Flavius Stilicho (360-408). His father was a Vandal cavalry officer who served the Emperor Valens (364-378), rose to high rank and married a Roman noblewoman. Since the reign of Diocletian (245–311), sons were obliged to follow their fathers' professions and so the young Stilicho

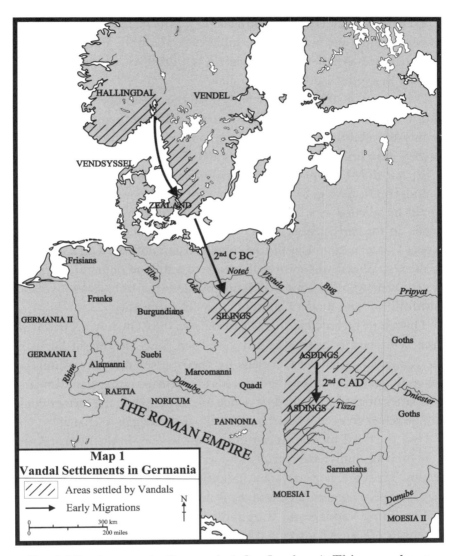

Vandal Settlements in Germania (after Jacobsen). This map shows
the gradual southern movements of the Vandals' ancestors from
Scandinavia to the first homeland between the Oder and Vistula rivers
and the subsequent migration of the Asdings into the Tisza basin.
The other named tribes show their approximate location in the
second-third centuries.

joined the Roman Army, entering the elite *protectores domestici* – a sort of combination bodyguard and staff officer cadre. By the time the Vandals crossed the Rhine in the early-fifth century, Stilicho had married into the Imperial family and held supreme military power in the Western Empire. Although he was half-Vandal in origin it is unlikely that Stilicho ever saw himself as anything other than Roman.

Other individual Vandals certainly filled the ranks of the Roman Army and fought faithfully for their new masters. It is difficult for us in the twenty-first century to understand the concepts of loyalty and nationality as they were understood 1,700 years ago. Then the nation state did not exist, nor did the concept of nationality as we now know it. Today, if a modern German goes off and fights for another nation or cause, he would be labelled as a mercenary or foreign fighter at best; terrorist at worst. In the early centuries AD there was no concept of a German or even a Vandal nation. Loyalty was personal and not based on nationality or race. A Vandal who swore allegiance to a Roman emperor, governor or centurion would see himself bound by sacred oaths to serve his leader faithfully without modern contradictions of nationality.

There is no recorded incident of a Vandal in the Roman Army betraying his new masters to the tribe he had come from. Since the time of Augustus the Romans had valued Germans for their personal loyalty. Emperors generally preferred to keep bodyguards of Germans rather than Romans. The latter might be tempted to switch allegiance while the former could still be relied on even when the political balance began to change.

Over the third and fourth centuries most Vandals in the Roman Army were probably individual recruits who served alongside others of different origins. There are, however, some indications that larger groups of Vandals may have been incorporated into the Roman Army to form distinct units.

The Siling Vandals and Burgundians who survived their defeat by Probus in 278 were conscripted into the Roman Army and sent to serve in Britain. Gervaisus of Tibury, who wrote the *Otia Imperialia* in 1214, says that there was a fortress called Wandlebria near modern Cambridge:

'In England, on the borders of the diocese of Ely, there is a town called Cantabrica, just outside of which is a place known as Wandlebria, from the fact that the Wandeli, when ravaging Britain and savagely putting to death the Christians, placed their camp there.'

There is indeed an ancient hill fort at Wandlebury Hill near Ely in Cambridgeshire which had been in use since the early Iron Age. There is archeological evidence that it was also occupied by the Romans. Given the name (and the fact that the German 'w' is pronounced as an English 'v') it could be that this fort was taken over by the Vandal soldiers serving in the Roman Army who later suppressed a local rebellion as recounted by Zosimus (quoted above). However, it is too far of a stretch to draw any firm conclusions from the name alone or from an unreliable thirteenth century account.

The *Notitia Dignitatum*, a list of offices and army units from the late-fourth/early-fifth century, records the *Ala VIII Vandilorum* serving in Egypt. An *Ala* was a cavalry unit of around 500 men at full strength. Given their name, it is most likely that they were originally made up by a majority of Vandals, even if later recruits may have been drawn from other sources. The fact that this was a cavalry unit may indicate an increasing preference for mounted warfare amongst some Vandals, if not all.

Early Vandal Warfare

By the time they had settled down as a warrior aristocracy in Roman Africa, the Vandals fought on horseback. Many of the eastern Germanic tribes who took up lands on the Eurasian steppe also, quite sensibly, became primarily mounted warriors. Being classed amongst the eastern Germanic peoples, it is usually assumed that the early Vandals had always tended to fight mounted rather than on foot.

Debating the ethnicity of a tribe he calls the 'Venedi', Tacitus says that they had adopted many Sarmatian habits. He then goes on to conclude that they were Germans because they 'carry shields and are fond of travelling fast on foot, differing in all these respects from the Sarmatians who live in wagons and on horseback.' For Tacitus, fighting on foot, as opposed to the mounted warfare of the nomadic Sarmatians, seems to have been a hallmark of the Germanic warrior in the early years of their contact with Rome. However, this was not absolute. Describing the Tencteri, whom he says lived by the Rhine, Tacitus asserts that they 'excel in skilful horsemanship', adding that even children and old men compete in riding and that horses are passed on to the most skilful warriors when a horse owner dies.

Mounted warfare naturally develops in open areas such as plains and steppes. Here a horse warrior has a natural advantage by being able to traverse greater distances at greater speed. Open plains also make raising and maintaining a substantial horse herd a relatively easy business. Neither the Vandals' original Scandinavian homeland, nor the mountainous, forested terrain of their new home in central Europe, would have been particularly suited to developing a horse culture. It is true that early Vandal burials contain horse furniture, but then most of the dead were cremated. Presumably only notable men were interred and the fact that they were the elite does not necessarily mean that all Vandal warriors were horsemen before their entry into the Roman Empire.

Fine distinctions between cavalry and infantry did not exist amongst the Germanic tribes. Warriors who had horses might fight mounted or dismount to fight on foot. Most of those who lived out on the steppes probably had horses. For others, like the early Vandals who lived in closer terrain, a horse would not have given the same tactical advantage and maintaining a suitable herd would have been much more difficult. Therefore, in the early days of Vandal history it is likely that only the richest men rode into battle and most probably even then dismounted to fight rather than forming a distinct cavalry force.

There are, however, several sources which seem to indicate a preference for mounted combat by the early Vandals. After their defeat by Aurelian in the 270s, the vanquished Sarmatians and Vandals were to provide 2,000 horsemen to the Roman Army. Probably most of these were Sarmatians but Vandals may have contributed. The *Ala VIII Vandilorum* previously mentioned was definitely a cavalry unit, which also supports the idea of a Vandal preference for mounted combat.

The terrain of the Vandal heartland in central Europe argues against the full development of mounted warfare in the early days of their history. Given the archeological evidence, it is likely that those who could afford it did own horses and most likely rode them into battle. The Asdings, who moved south into the Tisza basin, were clearly influenced by the Sarmatians, who were mounted nomads. Fighting alongside the Sarmatians, they would have come to value the strategic advantage that mounted action gave them for hit and run raids into enemy territory. The Hungarian plain would also have allowed them to build up larger horse herds than their Siling cousins to the north. Even if the Asdings had a greater number of mounted warriors than the Silings, it would probably be a mistake to imagine them as fighting exclusively on horseback as their descendants did in Africa several generations later.

Tacitus gives us some detailed descriptions of how the early Germans may have fought. Although these accounts contain a healthy dollop of poetic licence, they would have been based on first hand accounts of Roman officers who had fought against the Germans:

> 'Generally speaking, their strength lies in infantry rather than cavalry. So foot soldiers accompany the cavalry into action, their speed on foot being such that they can easily keep up with charging horsemen. The best men are chosen from the whole body of young warriors and placed with the cavalry in front of the main battle line...The battle line is made up of wedge shaped formations. To give ground, provided that you return to the attack, is considered good tactics rather than cowardice.'

The wedge shaped formations should not be taken too literally. The wedge, or *cuneus*, as it was called by the Romans, was more like an attack column with the leader front and centre surrounded by his household warriors. As the column surged forward, the leader and his best men would have advanced more quickly while those on the vulnerable flanks held back. By the time they reached the enemy, the formation would have resembled a rough wedge.

Tacitus says that the main weapons were short, handy spears called *frameae*. These have 'short and narrow blades which are sharp and easy to handle so that they can be used, as required, either at close quarters or in long range fighting. Their horsemen are content with a shield and a spear; but the foot soldiers also rain javelins on their foes. Each of them carries several and they hurl them to immense distances.'

When describing mounted action Tacitus says: 'Their horses are not remarkable for either their beauty or speed and are not trained to execute various evolutions as ours are. They ride them straight ahead, or with just a single wheel to the right (so the man's shielded side faces the enemy), keeping their line so well that not a man falls behind the rest.'

We have no way of knowing how much of this may have been applicable to the ancestors of the Vandals, of whom Tacitus had no knowledge. He does tell of tactical variations between certain tribes, one of whom were the Harii. This people were a sub-group of the Lugi who may have been later absorbed by the Vandals:

'The Harii are not only superior in strength to the other peoples I have mentioned, but they minister to their savage instincts by trickery and clever timing. They black their shields, dye their bodies, and choose pitch dark nights for their battles. The shadowy, awe-inspiring appearance of such a ghoulish army inspires mortal panic, for no enemy can endure a sight so strange and hellish. Defeat in battle starts always with the eyes.'

We cannot make any firm conclusions about the composition of early Vandal armies or their tactics. Probably they started off as mainly foot warriors like other Germans, but as terrain and circumstances permitted they increasingly mounted up. Notable warriors probably always rode into battle, even if they dismounted to fight on foot. As their wealth and power grew, Vandal warriors increasingly took to fighting on horseback, but at the time of the Rhine crossing many or most probably still fought on foot.

Whether on foot or mounted, the early Vandal warriors were much more likely to be involved in raids and skirmishes against their neighbours than large set piece battles. Most warbands would have numbered in the hundreds rather than thousands, and the objectives of a campaign would be to increase prestige and material wealth of that particular band as they jostled and competed for resources with other similar bands. If we were to take a modern comparison, it would be closer to rival street gangs fighting continuous turf wars rather than life or death conflicts between competing nations or ideologies.

Those warriors who fought dismounted may well have used a looser formation than the tight shieldwall typical of later Germanic warriors and the Romans. If hit-and-run raids were the most usual form of combat, relatively lightly-equipped men with the short handy spears and javelins described by Tacitus would have been most suited for it. Such men would have been able to operate easily in the close terrain of the Vandal homelands as well as keeping up with mounted warriors in the open. There is some archeological evidence to suggest that the

Germans of the early migration period may have had a looser fighting style than their later descendants. Shields were small, round and with prominent central bosses. This seems to indicate that the warrior's shield was used offensively and for parrying blows. Roman shields, and those of later Germans, were larger and better designed for defence in a close formation.

If Tacitus is correct, mounted action by the early Germans seems to have been rather unsophisticated. Romans, Sarmatians and Huns used a mix of skirmish and shock tactics. They would harass their opponents with missile weapons, avoiding contact until their enemy was worn down and then close in for the kill. Tacitus' statements that the Germans were 'not trained to execute various evolutions as ours are', and that, 'their horsemen are content with a shield and a spear (without javelins)', indicates a preference for close combat only. Later, when the Vandals fought the Moors and Romans in Africa, they seem to have been hampered by an inability to skirmish as well as fight hand-to-hand. It may be that Vandal mounted tactics did not evolve much over the centuries that followed.

Although there is a popular view that Germanic warriors shunned the use of missile weapons in favour of hand-to-hand combat only, there is plenty of evidence that this was not the case. Tacitus speaks of javelins being used by men on foot, their ability to fight at both close quarters or long range and the fact that a tactical withdrawal was not regarded as a sign of cowardice. The later Ostrogoths and Lombards fielded a large number of bow-armed men and several excavated Alamannic graves reveal that poorer warriors were buried with bows while richer ones had spears, swords and throwing axes.

As less prominent men amongst the early Vandals were cremated, we cannot know if the same was true for them. There is, however, no evidence for long-range missile weapons being used by the later Vandals, despite the influence of the Alans and Sarmatians who generally carried bows as well as lances. It may be that the Vandals never adopted archery. Perhaps, as they were so suddenly propelled from relatively minor tribes to a powerful warrior aristocracy, there was never a time when they had any significant number of less well-off men who had to make do with bows rather than the full panoply of the archetypical Germanic hand-to-hand fighter.

Amongst the early Germans, most free men carried arms and were able to fight. Even women and children might pitch in, taking care of the wounded and encouraging their menfolk:

'Close by them are their nearest and dearest, so that they can hear the shrieks of their women and the wailing of their children. These are the witnesses whom each man reverences most highly, whose praise he most desires. It is to their mothers and wives that they go to have their wounds treated and the women are not afraid to compare gashes. They also carry supplies of food to the combatants and encourage them.' (Tacitus)

Culture, Leadership and Society

Procopius, who wrote in the sixth century and was familiar with the later African Kingdom, tells us that the Vandals were closely related in language and laws to the Goths and Gepids:

'There were many Gothic nations in earlier times, just as also at the present, but the greatest and most important of all are the Goths, Vandals, Visigoths, and Gepids. In ancient times, however, they were named Sarmatians and Melanchlaeni [black cloaks – possibly a reference to Tacitus' Harii] and there were some too who called these nations Getic. All these, while they are distinguished from one another by their names, as has been said, do not differ in anything else at all. For they all have white bodies and fair hair, and are tall and handsome to look upon, and they use the same laws and practise a common religion. For they are all of the Arian faith, and have one language called Gothic; and, as it seems to me, they all came originally from one tribe, and were distinguished later by the names of those who led each group.'

Given the paucity of evidence it is difficult to identify any unique characteristics of early Vandal society beyond that which they shared with other German tribes. Archeology has identified cultural similarities amongst the peoples who lived in central Europe which differed from the Goths to the east, Marcomanni and Quadi to the south, and the Franks and Alamanni to the west. Although the early Vandals lived in central Europe, it is likely that their culture (known as 'Przeworsk' from the town in modern Poland where the first discoveries were made) was shared by several similar groups which included the Vandals. It was not necessarily exclusively theirs, and the fact that a common way of life extended over a wide area does not mean that the early Vandals were already a powerful confederacy in the years before the Rhine crossing.

What the archeology tells us is that the ancestors of the Vandals lived in small, highly-dispersed, short-lived communities based on subsistence farming. Their houses, made of wood, wicker and mud, were simple structures with one or two rooms. In contrast, those areas dominated by the Goths and Alamanni show signs of much larger permanent settlements with more advanced agricultural techniques and greater material wealth. This was no doubt a direct result of war and trade with Rome.

Trade with Rome would have been vitally important to the Vandals as it provided them with better quality goods and gave local leaders the ability to increase their power and influence. Although the Vandals were one step removed from the Imperial frontiers, their settlements straddled the so-called 'amber trail' so the Vandals did have something to offer in exchange for Roman luxury goods. Living deep in central Europe, most trade with Rome in the early years probably went through Marcomannic, Sarmatian or Gothic middlemen. As a result, the Vandals remained relatively poor and weak compared to their neighbours who bordered the Rhine and Danube.

Pre-migration Germanic leadership was fragile and fragmented. A successful warrior would offer material wealth and protection to his extended household and therefore attract more followers. Such Germanic leaders are usually called 'kings' by the Romans but they were not kings as we now understand the term. At best, such men were probably village headmen who, through prowess in war, were able to maintain a small number of household warriors and extend their influence over neighbouring settlements. There was no sense of a Vandal nation, nor even a Siling or Asding nation. In the same way that various South London gangs today can all be called Londoners, this does not mean that they automatically have some kind of greater allegiance to an overall London gang leader. Later, larger more coherent political groupings came about through military and economic interaction with Rome, but this did not come to pass for the Vandals until well after the Rhine crossing.

Interestingly, most primary sources mention two leaders when they describe the early Vandals. We have already heard how Ybor and Agio of the Lombards fought against Ambri and Assi of the Vandals; and how Raus and Raptus led their Asding followers into Dacia. This has led some historians to conclude that there was some kind of 'twin kingship' amongst the early Vandals and many other Germans. Tacitus seems to imply that this dual leadership was quite common, with one giving spiritual guidance while the other led warriors into battle. Dual leadership is also found in other cultures. After the death of King Rua, Attila and Bleda ruled the Huns jointly for several years until Attila did away with his brother to assume sole command. Given the fragmented nature of early Vandal political structures, it is probably wrong to assume that just because two leaders are often mentioned that this was always some sort of formal arrangement. It may well be that the two names were more symbolic than accurate. Tacitus, for example, links the dual kingship to the Roman divinities of Castor and Pollux, and the names 'Raus' and 'Raptus' may mean 'pole' and 'beam'.

As a single Vandal leader could probably only muster a few hundred men, only by joining up with another they could have had an impact that made a difference. As these 'kings' acquired greater wealth, often through their dealings with Rome, they were able to maintain larger groups of full-time retainers who were bound by formal oaths of loyalty and a code of honour. They fought for him to increase his power while he provided them with gifts, prestige and high standing within the community. In order to take on the might of Rome, several such leaders and their followings had to band together, at least temporarily, if they were to have any chance of success.

The Wrong Sort of Christians

If much of the early history of the Vandals will always remain shrouded in the mists of time, one event that is certain and had a lasting impact on their later history was their conversion to Christianity. This was significant less for the fact that they became Christians than that they adopted the Arian version of Christianity that was later deemed heretical by the Roman Church.

In 341 a Goth by the name of Ulfilas (Little Wolf) was consecrated Bishop at the Council of Antioch and was sent north of the Danube to bring his people around to Christianity. To say he was a Goth is true, but he is a good example of how ethnicity amongst the Germans was not necessarily based on race. He was descended from Roman captives taken by the Gothic Tervingi clan in the late-third century. He grew up as a Goth, had a Gothic name and spoke Gothic as his first language, but he was also fluent in Latin and Greek, and he retained his parents' Christian beliefs.

Ulfilas translated the Bible into Gothic and gradually converted his people to Christianity. His work, and that of his followers, influenced other Germanic tribes as the word spread beyond Gothic territory. As neighbours of the Goths, the Vandals probably converted to Christianity towards the end of the fourth century as an indirect result of Ulfilas' mission.

The fifth-century Spanish chronicler Orosius says that the Vandals were still heathens when they crossed the Rhine in 406-7, but this is highly unlikely. By the time they arrived in Spain, the Vandals were almost certainly Christians. Conversion needs time to contemplate spiritual matters and this is not easily done while you are marauding through enemy territory. Given their proximity to the Goths and similar dialect, it is far more likely that the Vandals became Christians before the Rhine crossing. Had it happened later they would have taken on the Catholic version of Christianity of the Hispano-Romans rather than following the Arian teachings of Ulfilas.

Today, in the West, we tend to think of religion as a personal matter where each individual makes up his or her own mind independently. In late antiquity this was not the case. Shared beliefs were then an important part of the tribe's identity. If your leaders decided that Christianity was the way of the future, then you would follow suit. In post-Reformation Germany, small principalities and even clusters of villages often switched between Catholicism and Protestantism in accordance with their leaders' decisions. The same was probably true of the Vandals. If Ulfilas' priests could convince the elite, then the rest of the people would convert alongside them. Early Germanic leaders were not autocrats, so they would need to take their followers' views into consideration. It helped greatly that the early Christians were quite happy to adopt pagan festivals and practices by giving them a patron saint or a Christian gloss so that life could go on more or less as it had in the past. Once the Vandals converted to Christianity, this belief became part of what made up the Vandal identity. This should have made integration with the Christian Roman world easier, but there was a problem.

Ulfilas followed the teachings of the Bishop Arius (250–336), which in the early part of the fourth century were fairly widely accepted. In simple layman's terms, Arius believed that Jesus was a man created by God the Father. He was from God but Jesus and the Father were not the same being. Others held that the Trinity of the Father, Son and Holy Ghost were one and the same with no differentiation or hierarchy between them. This is necessarily a very simplistic interpretation. The subtle nuances surrounding the nature of the Trinity resulted in the deaths of thousands of believers on both sides as the various adherents of one idea or the other persecuted their opponents with fanatical fervour. The Council of Nicaea in 325 attempted to draw a line under the controversy, defining the relationship of the Son and Father as 'of the same substance'. As a result the idea that the Father, Son and Holy Ghost were the same being became known as the Nicene Belief, and from this we get the Nicene Creed which is today still the official doctrine of the Catholic Church.

The Nicaean Council did not settle the matter. Furious, frequently deadly debates continued as the East Roman Empire became consumed with the relationship between Jesus and God. At a second Ecumenical Council at Constantinople in 381, the Arian version that the Son and Father were similar, but not the same, was finally declared heretical. The Nicene Creed became the only acceptable interpretation of Christianity and the matter was finally settled.

Or was it?

No one bothered to invite the Vandals to the councils at Nicaea or Constantinople. While a new orthodoxy had been accepted by Christians within the Roman Empire, those beyond the frontiers still held firm to the Arian version as preached by Ulfilas and his followers. In the years that followed, integration between Nicene Romans and Arian Germans was problematic to say the least. In the case of the Vandals these difficulties were even more pronounced.

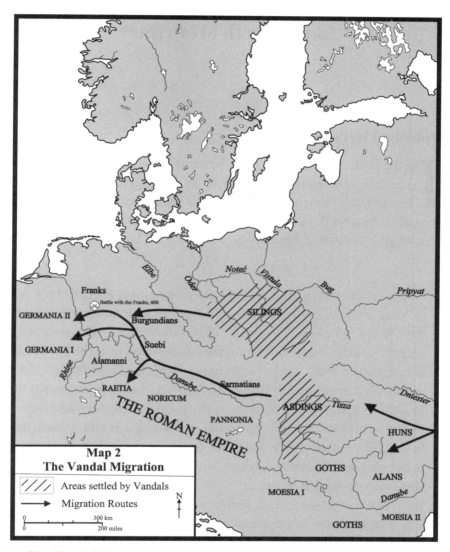

The Vandal Migration in the fifth century (after Jacobsen). Under
pressure from the Huns, the Vandals moved west at the beginning
of the fifth century. A group of Asdings moved into Raetia in 401 but
were defeated by Stilicho. In 406 the Asdings and Silings moved into
Frankish territory, joined by groups of Suevi and Alans along the way.
After a battle with the Franks, the migrants crossed the Rhine on
31 December 406.

Chapter 2

In the Bleak Midwinter

Upheaval Beyond the Frontiers

In the mid-fourth century the Germanic tribes beyond the Roman frontiers were thrown into disarray by new migrants from the east. The Huns, a nomadic people living on the Eurasian steppes, started expanding westward. In two separate passages, the fourth century Roman officer and historian, Ammianus Marcellinus, has this to say about them:

'The seed and origin of all the ruin and various disasters that the wrath of Mars aroused, putting in turmoil all places with unwonted fires, we have found to be this. The people of the Huns, but little known from ancient records, dwelling beyond the Maeotic Sea near the ice-bound ocean, exceed every degree of savagery. The cheeks of their children are deeply furrowed with steel from their very birth, in order that the growth of hair, when it appears at the proper time, may be checked by the wrinkled scars, they grow old without beards and without any beauty, like eunuchs. They all have compact, strong limbs and thick necks, and are so monstrously ugly and misshapen, that one might take them for two-legged beasts...

'When the report spread widely among the other Gothic peoples, that a race of men hitherto unknown had now arisen from a hidden nook of the earth, like a tempest of snows from the high mountains, and was seizing or destroying everything in its way, the greater part of the people, who, worn out by lack of the necessities of life... looked for a home removed from all knowledge of the savages.'

The impact of Hun expansion had a domino effect on the tribes of ancient Germania. Some were conquered and absorbed into the Hun Empire, whilst others moved further west looking for new lands where they might still remain free. Like water building up behind an inadequate dam, a huge conglomeration of displaced Germanic peoples flooded into the Roman Empire from the late-fourth to early-fifth centuries.

The Huns seem to have come west in two waves. The first was in the mid-fourth century when they moved against the Alans and Goths, who at the time were living north of the Black Sea. The Goths and Alans were defeated and some came under Hun control. Two Gothic bands, the Tervingi and some Gruethungi, fled further west and sought refuge inside the Roman Empire.

The first Gothic refugees were allowed to cross the border but the unscrupulous behaviour of local Roman officials, combined with the closing of the frontier to new arrivals, sparked off a rebellion. The end result was the famous destruction of the East Roman Army and the death of the Emperor Valens at Adrianople in 378. As he was a cavalry officer serving Valens, it may be that Stilicho's Vandal father fought on the Roman side at Adrianople, but we have no direct evidence for this.

The events of the 370s are beautifully and succinctly summed up by Bishop Ambrose of Milan in a style that brings to mind a modern 'Tweet': 'The Huns fell upon the Alans, the Alans upon the Goths and Taifali, the Goths and Taifali upon the Romans, and yet this is not yet the end.'

How right he was.

The story of the Goths will be told more fully in the next book in this series. The end result was that after four years of inconclusive campaigning, the Goths and Romans looked for a negotiated settlement. On 3 October 382 a treaty was agreed which gave the Goths land to settle on the southern bank of the Danube. In return for this and a semi-autonomous status within the Empire, the Goths were to provide troops for the Roman Army. On the face of it this was nothing really new. Barbarians had long been employed in the Roman Army and there was a history of settling defeated tribes as military colonists. The treaty of 382 may have seemed similar, but the reality was different. The Goths were not defeated and an entire people were now settled inside the Empire, remaining under their own laws and fighting as a distinct entity under their own leaders.

Twilight of Empire

As the fourth century drew to a close the centre of Hun power was still to the east of the Carpathian Mountains, while the Danube border regions remained occupied by Germans and Sarmatians. The Vandals do not appear to have been particularly unsettled by the first Hun attacks and there is no mention of Vandals taking part in any of the Gothic incursions of the 370s.

Before continuing our narrative of the Vandals, it is worth examining the political and military situation in the Roman Empire at the turn of the fourth century. Only then can we begin to understand how the seemingly impossible occurred.

The defeat of the East Roman Army at Adrianople was a catastrophe, but as the fourth century drew to a close it seemed on the surface that Constantinople had managed to stabilise the situation. The Goths were more or less settled in the Balkans, providing manpower for the army. The Huns had made their presence known but were not yet pushing up against Rome's borders. An equilibrium seemed to have been established beyond the frontiers. The Emperor Theodosius maintained a strong grip and was busy building a new Christian Empire. Things should have been looking up, but with the benefit of hindsight we can see that the Empire's situation was highly precarious.

In 382, Magnus Maximus (Macsen Wledig of Welsh legend) was proclaimed Emperor by his British troops. With the backing of soldiers drawn from Britain and never to return, he defeated the Western Emperor Gratian, established his capital at Trier and for six years controlled the West. He was eventually defeated by Theodosius' Eastern army in 388. The Theodosian forces included a sizeable contingent of Goths, while Maximus drew on the Alamanni as well as the British and Gallic garrisons. Drawing off troops from Gaul to fight Theodosius in Italy left the Rhine frontier sparsely defended and, in a harbinger of things to come, the Franks took advantage of this to move into northern Gaul and establish settlements on the west bank of the Rhine.

After Maximus' defeat, the political situation in the West remained precarious. In 392, the new, youthful Western Emperor Valentinian II attempted to dismiss Arbogast, his *Magister Militum* (master of soldiers).

The result was that Valentinian died in rather dubious circumstances and Arbogast (of Frankish origin) placed his puppet Eugenius on the western throne.

This perturbed Theodosius on several accounts. The greatest was perhaps that Arbogast and Eugenius were pagans and there were signs that they might be encouraging a pagan revival. Once again Theodosius decided that he had to intervene to sort things out and once again he called on the Goths to back him. Some sources say the Goths provided 20,000 men, but such a large number is highly unlikely. Together with the Goths and reinforcements from Syria, Theodosius and his general, the half-Vandal Stilicho, marched west in September 394 to defeat Arbogast in a two-day battle that took place in a mountain pass in modern Slovenia through which the River Frigidus flows (modern Vipava in Slovenian or Vipacco in Italian).

Theodosius' victory over Arbogast was won with the blood of many Goths. Alaric, their leader, then sought some better understanding for future relations. Ideally he was looking for formal recognition for himself and his followers within the Roman military and political structure. The full narrative of Alaric and Stilicho belongs to the story of the Goths. As far as it concerns the story of the Vandals, the important point is that Stilicho was primarily focused on the political situation within the Empire rather than what was going on beyond the Rhine frontier.

After Frigidus, Stilicho became guardian of Theodosius's 9-year-old son, Honorius, whom he had placed on the Western throne. When Theodosius died in 395 his eldest, 17-year-old son, Arcadius, ascended to the Eastern throne. As the vultures circled around the two young emperors, Stilicho held supreme military power. His only real rival was Alaric, who had become increasingly dissatisfied with being bottled up in the Balkans without a clear agreement about his official status as a Roman warlord.

As the fifth century dawned, Stilicho had his gaze firmly fixed on Alaric in the Balkans and Arcadius in Constantinople. The western Rhine frontier seemed immaterial to the more important and inevitable struggle to follow. Many of the troops previously stationed in Britain and Gaul had been drawn off, first to support Maximus and then to provide manpower for Arbogast and Eugenius. Settlements of Franks, Alamanni and Burgundians were engaged to hold the Rhine to replace the Roman forces drawn off to deal with other more pressing matters. When Alaric rebelled in 401, Stilicho withdrew more troops from the West to defend Italy from Alaric's Goths.

We have a reasonably good idea of the theoretical strength and dispositions of the Roman Army from the *Notitia Dignitatum*. On paper the combined might of the two halves of the Empire could muster something close to half a million men. In the West there were two main field armies; one under the *Magister Peditum* in Italy and another in Gaul under the *Magister Equitum*. These had an official strength of around 25,000 men each. These field armies were mobile forces of high quality troops, who could respond in force to deal with major threats while more static forces guarded the frontiers. The main frontier forces in the West were located in Britain, Illyricum (modern former Yugoslavia), Africa and along the Rhine and Danube frontiers. In theory this should have provided more than enough men to defeat incursions by the relatively small barbarian armies that from time to time raided across the frontiers. If the garrison forces along the borders were unable to hold the enemy, then the field armies would intervene. After defeating their opponents they would often conduct punitive expeditions into barbarian territory to deter future aggression.

This system had worked reasonably well in the fourth century but it was unable to cope with the perfect storm that engulfed the Empire in the first decade of the fifth century. We have already seen how Maximus, then Arbogast, and finally Stilicho drew troops away from Britain and Gaul to either support their bids for power or to defend Italy. These troops never returned to their home stations, nor were new units recruited to replace them. Instead, Stilicho established treaties with the Franks and Alamanni to secure the Rhine frontier, while Saxons were invited into Britain to help defend the island from the Scots and Picts.

The Gathering Storm

At some point at the end of the fourth century or beginning of the fifth, the Huns moved westward again. They occupied the Hungarian plain and sent a new wave of refugees up against the Roman frontiers. This time the Vandals were amongst them. Led by Godegisel, the Asdings were probably the first to move and some were pushing up against the Danube and raiding into Raetia as early as 401. These early Vandal raiders were defeated by Stilicho and some of the survivors may have been engaged as *foederati* (federates), given land in exchange for military service.

It is worth pausing for a moment to consider just how momentous a decision it must have been for the Vandals to up-sticks and move. Despite their later wanderings, the Vandals were settled farmers and not nomads. They had lived in more or less the same part of central Europe for hundreds of years and by migrating westward they would leave everything that was familiar behind forever.

The decision would not have been taken lightly, nor quickly. Around the council fires there must have been many voices arguing to stay put and come to some sort of accord with the Huns. Other Germanic peoples, such as the Gepids, did take that option and in the end seem to have done fairly well by it. It may be that the decision to move was influenced by other factors than simply terror at the approach of the Huns. In all likelihood some warriors decided to strike out early, like those who raided Raetia in 401, then as conditions worsened others made the move, taking their families with them.

Procopius, writing in the sixth century, attributes the Vandal migration to famine. Perhaps there had been several poor harvests which made staying put in face of the advancing Huns a less than promising option. It is also interesting to note that Procopius also says that not all the Vandals migrated: 'When the Vandals originally pressed by hunger, were about to remove from their ancestral abodes, a certain part of them was left behind who were reluctant to go and not desirous of following Godegisel.'

It is generally assumed that, unlike the Goths, all the Vandals – both Silings and Asdings, men, women and children – migrated west in the early fifth century. Archeology tends to back this up. Material goods connected with the so-called Przeworsk culture have been found in the Vandals' central European heartland dating back centuries. Then, suddenly, from the start of the fifth century these artefacts disappear from the archeological record entirely. It may be that there was a split as Procopius says and that the end of the Przeworsk culture could be accounted for by the warrior elites moving on, leaving the others behind to fall under Hun overlordship or be absorbed by other tribes. We cannot know for certain but on balance it would seem as though most, if not all, Vandals moved west to seek a new home inside the Roman Empire. This would not have been a coordinated migration but rather decisions made by individual groups, with some moving earlier and others joining in later. As each group made their decision, they would have had to weigh up the difficulties of their present situation against the possibility of a better life in the future.

What realistic hope did the Vandals have of carving out new lands for themselves inside the Empire? Most barbarian incursions into Roman territory were doomed to failure. They might achieve initial success but eventually the Romans would prevail, destroying the invaders and following up with punitive raids against their homelands. The aftermath of Adrianople in 378 had broken this mould. When the Vandals were contemplating their options they would have been well aware that the descendants of the Gothic victors at Adrianople had both land and status within the Empire. The Franks had also been granted land on the west bank of the Rhine in exchange for military service, and all the tribes along the Rhine frontier – Franks, Burgundians and Alamanni – had done quite well out of recent treaties with Stilicho.

The Vandals must have thought that they too could hope for a similar arrangement, especially if the man in charge, Stilicho, was himself a Vandal on his father's side. Jordanes goes as far as to say that the Vandals were invited into the Empire by Stilicho:

'A long time afterward they [the Vandals] were summoned thence [to Gaul] by Stilicho, Master of the Soldiery, Ex-Consul and Patrician, and took possession of Gaul. Here they plundered their neighbours and had no settled place of abode.'

Could there be any truth to this claim?

Gaul had been a thorn in Stilicho's side for years. It was the place where rivals could and did rise up to challenge him and the Emperor Honorius, whom he protected. His interest was in maintaining his power base in Italy, keeping an eye on Alaric's Goths in the Balkans and playing politics with Constantinople. The Gallic Army had been decimated in the civil wars of the late-fourth century, and in 401 Stilicho withdrew more troops from Gaul to support his struggle against Alaric's Goths who were threatening Italy. While the Rhine defences needed bolstering, the last thing Stilicho wanted was another strong Gallic Army to challenge him.

Therefore it is not beyond the realm of possibility that he would have been tempted to have his Vandal cousins move into Gaul as his surrogates. Even if Stilicho had not formally invited the Vandals, maybe there had been communications which some Vandal leaders had interpreted as an invitation, even if they were only meant as polite diplomatic words.

Virtually all modern historians discount collusion between Stilicho and the Vandals, despite the former's ancestry and despite the fact that he did very little to oppose their crossing into Gaul. The Vandals were not the only barbarians on the move. Goths, Suevi, Alans and others were forced out of their central European homelands by the Huns, famine or both in the first years of the fifth century. Even when the Vandals crossed the Rhine, they were probably a minority partner to the Suevi and Alans. Furthermore, Stilicho's policy had been to rely on the Franks and other western Germanic tribes to secure the Rhine for him in place of Roman soldiers. This policy seemed to have worked relatively well and there would have been no reason for him to change it. In the unlikely event that there had been any understanding between Stilicho and some of the Vandal leaders, the chain of events in the first decade of the fifth century were so cataclysmic to overwhelm all involved.

All of a sudden hundreds of thousands of people were willingly or unwillingly on the move, and the Vandals were only a small part of this movement. Most probably the decisions to migrate were sparked off by the westward expansion of the Huns, but no doubt many other factors came into play as well. These may have included food shortages, although the climatic records from around 400 do not reveal any unusual weather patterns. Probably there was also a degree of opportunism on the part of the Vandals, Suevi and Alans, as they saw how Stilicho was otherwise occupied and knew that the Rhine defences were relatively thin.

As the Huns migrated from the Eurasian steppes into central Europe, the first wave of displaced Germans to break over the Roman frontier was led by Radagasius, a Goth, who brought a large army into Italy in 405. The composition of Radagasius' force is not known but probably it was a coalition of various Germanic peoples, possibly including some Asding Vandals. It included women and children as well as warriors, so it was a migration rather than a raiding force. Radagasius' force was large enough to require Stilicho to call on thirty units from the Roman field army as well as Hun and Alan auxiliaries to oppose him. He also withdrew yet more troops from the Rhine frontier to bolster Italy's defences. This probably gave Stilicho something in the region of 20–25,000 men.

It is interesting to note that, according to the *Notitia Dignitatum*, the Italian field army contained seven cavalry and thirty-seven infantry units in the fifth century, with another twelve cavalry and forty-eight infantry units in the Gallic Army. These were on top of the border troops stationed along the frontiers. Yet it took a great deal of time and effort to gather the thirty units needed to oppose Radagasius, leaving the invaders plenty of time to ravage northern Italy while Stilicho marshalled his forces. This is good example of just how misleading official army organizational lists can be. Unit strengths and levels of readiness can vary hugely and often only a tiny fraction of the theoretical military capability can be deployed. This remains a problem even in the modern world. If we think of the huge efforts it took by NATO nations and others to maintain relatively small numbers of troops in Afghanistan to deal with insurgents, then we have some idea of the problems facing the Romans in the fifth century.

In the end, Stilicho decisively defeated Radagaisus near Florence on 23 August 406. Then he fixed his attention firmly on the east, oblivious or unaware of the storm gathering to the north and west.

The Storm Breaks

The coalition of Asding and Siling Vandals, together with Alans and Suevi, crossed the Rhine on 31 December 406. This is the date given by Prosper of Aquitaine. In recent years some historians have made a case for the crossing taking place a year earlier – that is on 31 December 405. This is partly based on the fact that Zosimus says that the ravaging of Gaul took place in 406 and it is unlikely he would have assigned that year if the barbarians only crossed on the last day of it. Also in 406 there were a number of usurpations in Britain and these are often seen as a reaction to the lack of response to the invasion of Gaul by the Imperial authorities. To make matters more confusing, Orosius says that the Rhine crossing took place two years before the Gothic sack of Rome, which would be 408.

I am not particularly convinced by the arguments for shifting the occasion of the Rhine crossing and therefore prefer to stick with the rather precise date Prosper has given us of New Year's Eve 406. But before trying to reconstruct the actual Rhine crossing itself, we should look at what was happening in the months that led up to it.

By the end of 405, Stilicho had defeated Radagasius and incorporated 12,000 of the survivors into his army, while others dispersed to join Alaric's Goths in the Balkans and the westward-moving Vandals. In 406, a series of revolts took place in Britain with the British Army proclaiming Marcus and Gratian in quick succession as Emperor before assassinating their candidates when they did not do as the army wished. Towards the end of 406, the British Army settled on a soldier with the suitably Imperial name of Constantine (Constantine III), who managed to retain their approval. Meanwhile Stilicho became embroiled in a fight with Constantinople over control of the Balkans. Parts of the Balkan provinces had previously belonged to the Western Empire but had been transferred to the East several years earlier. Stilicho wanted them back as they were a prime recruiting ground for soldiers. Additionally, it would give him territory he could offer to Alaric in order to finally come to a lasting and peaceful settlement with his troublesome Goths.

Meanwhile, the Vandals had been moving slowly westward as part of a greater movement of displaced peoples. After the failure of Radagasius' migration across the Danube, the southern route into the Roman Empire had to be ruled out, leaving the Rhine frontier as their only hope. If we discount any collusion with Stilicho, it is unlikely that the Vandals had detailed intelligence of the state of Roman defences along the west bank of the Rhine, just as Stilicho was apparently unaware of the large westward movements beyond the frontier. This does, of course, call into question whether or not there may have been some collusion.

The problem for the Vandals was that if the west bank of the Rhine may have been relatively weakly defended, the east bank was not. The powerful Alemannic and Frankish confederacies were well established on the upper and lower Rhine respectively, with the Burgundians edging into the gap between them. These tribes had been in long contact with Rome and had benefited from it. Their societies had greater material wealth than the Vandals, more developed organizational structures and they were being subsidized by Rome to hold the Rhine frontier. The last thing they would have welcomed would have been a new group of illegal immigrants knocking on their door for a piece of the action.

Unsurprisingly, the arrival of the Vandal migrants led to conflict as the Franks and Alamanni attempted to close their borders. There were probably many small engagements as groups of new immigrants tried their luck, only to be repulsed. Most of these have gone unrecorded, but at some point there was a major battle between the Vandals and the Franks. Fragments of the contemporary writer Renatus Profuturus Frigeridus, preserved by Gregory of Tours, say that the Vandals were on the brink of a catastrophic defeat. Their king, Godegisel, was killed in the fighting but at the last minute the Vandals were saved by the timely intervention of a force of Alans under Respendial, who 'turned the army of his people from the Rhine, since the Vandals were getting the worse of the war with the Franks, having lost their king, Godegisel, and about 20,000 of the army, and all the Vandals would have been exterminated if the army of the Alans had not come to their aid in time.'

This battle probably took place some time in the summer or autumn of 406, and it allowed the Vandals and their allies to move into Frankish territory on the middle Rhine. Although they had won a path to the Roman frontier, the new immigrants must have been in a fairly desperate state. Unable to grow or harvest crops and with no supply bases to call on, it would have been a monumental task to keep their people and livestock alive. The Vandals were a settled people with no nomadic history and no expertise in living off the land. If they managed to move up to the Rhine in the autumn of 406 they may have been able to take in some of the crops the Franks had planted, but this would at best only keep starvation at bay for a few months.

In the pre-industrial age armies rarely moved in a North European winter. Without the benefit of canned goods, mass production and mechanised transport that did not require forage, any movement of a large group of people in winter would inevitably lead to utter disaster. Yet the Asdings, Silings, Suevi and Alans crossed the Rhine in the depths of midwinter. What on earth persuaded them to do this when all sensible armies would have been in winter quarters awaiting the onset of the spring campaigning season?

The traditional view is that the winter was so cold that the Rhine froze over, giving the invaders the possibility to cross on a wide front. Although the Rhine remains open all year round in present times, it has frozen over in the past and it is not impossible that it froze in the winter of 406/7. Whether the ice would have been thick enough for tens of thousands of people with their wagons and baggage to cross is another matter. There are no contemporary accounts to support the idea of a crossing on ice, despite the fact that it has become a relatively accepted popular image.

The most evocative popular account of the crossing of the frozen Rhine is in Wallace Breem's delightful novel *Eagle in the Snow*. Here we see the last remnants of the Roman frontier forces fighting a last stand, which is doomed as soon as the Rhine freezes. A story of civilization fighting off barbarism or established cultures digging in against impoverished migrants has a strong resonance today, just as it did in the eighteenth century when Edward Gibbon wrote his *Decline and Fall of the Roman Empire*. It was Gibbon who first gave us the story of the Rhine freezing over, possibly to explain his incomprehension at how the Vandals, Alans and Suevi were able to cross over into Gaul with such apparent ease. Many modern writers have followed Gibbon, although even he himself was not definitive about the river freezing: 'On the last day of the year, in a season when the waters of the Rhine were *most probably frozen* [my italics], they entered, without opposition, the defenceless provinces of Gaul.'

In truth, the move of tens of thousands of people with all their belongings in the depths of midwinter must have been one of desperation. The Frankish lands the migrants had occupied on the east bank would not have sustained them for long. As winter began to set in, so would the prospect of starvation. On the west bank there were well-provisioned towns and a few probing raids would have given the Vandals and their allies some indication of the paucity of Roman defences, which had been stripped to support Stilicho's campaigns in Italy.

The crossing of the Rhine probably took place at several points, with Mainz (Mogontiacum) as the centre of axis. It did not need the Rhine to freeze over to make such a crossing possible. The Roman Rhine bridges were still standing, and if the river was open then picked warriors in makeshift boats could have gone across first to secure the bridgeheads. If the river had frozen over then this could possibly have been done over the ice. If there was even partial freezing of the river, then the Roman Rhine fleet would not have been able to intervene.

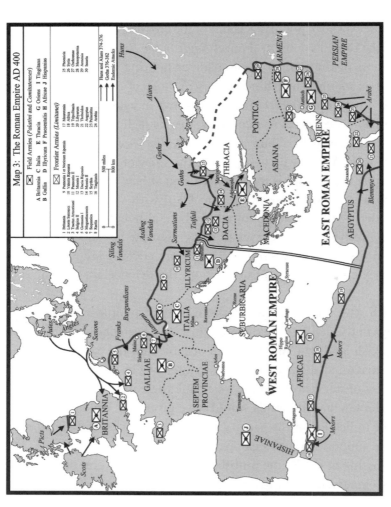

The Defence of the Roman Empire AD 400. This shows the major administrative divisions of the Roman Empire and the location of her armies according to the *Notitia Dignitatum* at the beginning of the fifth century. It also shows the movements of the barbarians up to the Gothic treaty with Theodosius in 382.

Defending the Rhine

In order to understand how easily the Vandals, Alans and Suevi crossed the Rhine once they had defeated the Franks on the east bank, we need to appreciate the Roman system of defence. The frontiers, were defended by troops deployed in fortifications along the borders of the empire. Known as *limitanei* (soldiers defending the frontiers, or *limes*) or *riparienses* (soldiers defending the rivers), these men occupied strongpoints along the frontiers and patrolled the borders. Deployed in relatively small detachments, they were able to deter or intervene to deal with small-scale incursions but were neither expected nor able to deal with a major invasion. To think of them in modern terms, they were more like a border force or home guard than regular armed forces, even though many of the units could trace their heritage back to the legions of previous centuries. Backing them up, in the Western Empire, there were two main field armies, one based in Italy and the other in Gaul. Each of these field armies were, on paper, about 20-30000 strong and it was their job to intervene once the frontiers has been breached to defeat the invaders and restore order. The field army units were known as *palatini* – the most senior units who were originally part of a central army commanded in person by the Emperor – and *comitatenses* – units of the regional field armies. Units of *limitanei* drawn from the frontier to reinforce the field armies took on the title of *pseudocomitatenses*.

This was the theoretical principle of defence, but in reality the field armies in the fifth century were more occupied supporting various political interests than they were in defending the empire from external threats. Stilicho had the support of the Italian field army but not that of Gaul. When Constantine crossed over from Britain in early 407, the Gallic Army went over to him.

The Gallic field army was commanded by the *Magister Equitum intra Gallias* who in theory had twelve cavalry and forty-eight infantry units at his disposal, with unit strengths probably averaging out at roughly 500 men each. However, we have already seen how Stilicho struggled to field an army of thirty units to fight Radagasius and so we should not assume that the *Magister Equitum's* entire force could be quickly and easily deployed. Furthermore, many of these units would have been severely weakened after their defeat in the civil wars and may well not have been anything like at full strength.

The defence of the middle Rhine, where the Vandals crossed, fell to the *Dux Mogontiacensis* (Duke of Mainz). According to the *Notitia Dignitatum*, he had eleven prefects under his command. The units commanded by these prefects and their home stations are recorded as:

Praefectus militum Pacensium, at Saletio (Seltz)
Praefectus militum Menapiorum, at Tabernae (Rheinzabern)
Praefectus militum Anderetianorum, at Vicus Julius (Germersheim)
Praefectus militum Vindicum, at Nemetes (Speyer)
Praefectus militum Martensium, at Alta Ripa (Altrip)
Praefectus militum Secundae Flaviae, at Vangiones (Worms)
Praefectus militum Armigerorum, at Mogontiacum (Mainz)
Praefectus militum Bingensium, at Vingo (Bingen)
Praefectus militum Balistariorum, at Bodobrica (Boppard)
Praefectus militum Defensorum, at Confluentes (Koblenz)
Praefectus militum Acincensium, at Antennacum (Andernach)

Some of these units are also listed under the Gallic field army, which may indicate that they had been pulled back from the Rhine. Alternatively, it could also mean that a few units of the field army such as the *Menapii* and *Armigeri* (senior legions of the Gallic field army and also listed under the *Dux Mogontiacensis*) had been sent to reinforce the frontier. However, as the trend had been to strip the frontiers to bolster the field armies it seems that the first possibility is the most likely.

These units probably only contained few hundred men each. While they could hold the walls of a fortified strongpoint and mount patrols, there could never have been any possibility that these dispersed garrisons could block a crossing of the frontier by many thousand warriors, even if the latter were weakened by hunger and bogged down with their families and chattels. At best all these men could hope for would be to hold out behind their fortifications while the barbarians moved past, to be dealt with by the field army at a later date.

There was also a Rhine fleet, the *Classis Germanica*, which patrolled the river and was an integral part of the Roman defensive system. We do not know how large it was, but in 359 Ammianus Marcellinus tells us that a squadron of forty ships was used against the Alamanni. Later inscriptions testify to ongoing clashes with Germanic tribes up until the Rhine crossing in 406. If the Rhine had been frozen or partially frozen, then it would have prevented any ships from intercepting the invaders. The *Classis Germanica* seems to have disappeared after the Vandal invasion as there is no mention of it in the *Notitia Dignitatum*.

So if the *Dux Mogontiacensis* and his border force were never expected to hold back a major invasion, what did the Gallic field army do?

Apparently very little.

In the fourth century the Gallic capital had been at Trier on the Rhine, but by the fifth century it had moved to Arles at the mouth of the Rhone in the south. The Rhine had been abandoned psychologically, if not yet in reality. From Arles, the focus of the authorities was far more towards Italy and the Mediterranean than to the northern frontiers.

The explanation for the apparent inaction by the Gallic Army rests in the convoluted Imperial politics of the time. On paper the Gallic Army should have had enough men to deal with the barbarian incursion across the Rhine. However, as the Vandals and their allies were crossing into Gaul from Germany, so too was Constantine from Britain. Unloved and run down by Stilicho, the Gallic Army threw in their lot with Constantine and their main worry was to hold their own against the Imperial authorities with the barbarian incursion a secondary concern.

Constantine probably crossed the channel in early 407, bringing with him the last remnants of the Roman Army in Britain. He forged alliances with the Franks and Alamanni and there is some evidence that he fought against the various bands of Vandals, Suevi and Alans to bottle them up in northern Gaul for a while.

Most of the military might of the Western Empire resided under Stilicho's command in Italy. He was about to embark on a war with the Eastern Empire over control of Illyricum. So what did he do when he learned that the barbarians were overrunning Gaul and that Constantine was doing his best to contain them?

Naturally he did what any late Roman potentate would do. He sent an army to Gaul to destroy Constantine. A usurper was, after all, a far greater threat to his power than a mere barbarian invasion. Stilicho's army, led by the Goth Sarus, was defeated, leaving Constantine in control of Britain and Gaul, with Spain also recognizing his authority. So it was, that rather than concentrating their forces to defeat a foreign invader the

Romans fought amongst themselves and left the field open to the Vandals and their allies.

A Funeral Pyre

In this age of Twitter and 24/7 news, we could be forgiven for thinking that we have invented the art of the short soundbite. However, the ancient Romans were just as happy as we are to condense complex ideas to 140 characters or less. So it is that the poet Orientius gives us a wonderful line that encapsulates the impact of the Vandal migration: 'All Gaul was filled with the smoke of a single funeral pyre.'

Deconstructing exactly what happened to create this funeral pyre is difficult, if not impossible.

In all likelihood, the Vandals, Suevi and Alans crossed the Rhine on a fairly wide front, with Mainz as their main crossing point. It is the first town mentioned by St Jerome (see quote below) and there was a good Roman bridge over the river at this point, the remains of which can still be seen today. Mainz was near the southernmost boundary of Frankish-held territory, after which there was a stretch of river under contention. Further south the Alamanni held sway, while the Burgundians were pushing into the buffer zone between them. After defeating the Franks in the summer of 406, the Vandals and their allies would naturally have moved into the contested border regions. As winter set in, bringing the prospect of starvation, they would have been well aware that Mainz, just over the river, was well stocked with provisions.

Mainz possibly fell without a fight, the garrison of the *Praefectus militum Armigerorum* either fleeing or having already been withdrawn before the crossing took place. As the *Armigeri* (*Armigeri Defensores Seniores*) are also listed in the Gallic field army, the latter may well have been the case. After capturing Mainz, the Vandals would have been able to supply themselves and contemplate moving on beyond the frontier, where the towns had no garrisons at all. St Jerome lists the towns that fell to the barbarians in an evocative letter written in 409 in which he warns of the coming of the Antichrist:

'Savage tribes in countless numbers have overrun all parts of Gaul. The whole country between the Alps and the Pyrenees, between the

Rhine and the Ocean, has been laid waste by hordes of Quadi, Vandals, Sarmatians, Alans, Gepids, Heruls, Saxons, Burgundians, Alamanni and – alas for the commonweal—even hostile Pannonians. For "Assur also is joined with them."

'The once noble city of Mainz has been captured and destroyed. In its church many thousands have been massacred. The people of Worms after standing a long siege have been extirpated. The powerful city of Rheims, the Ambiani, the Altrebatae (Amiens and Arras), the Belgians on the skirts of the world, Tournay, Speyer, and Strasbourg have fallen to the Germans: while the provinces of Aquitaine and of the Nine Nations, of Lyons and of Narbonne are with the exception of a few cities one universal scene of desolation. And those which the sword spares without, famine ravages within. I cannot speak without tears of Toulouse which has been kept from failing hitherto by the merits of its reverend bishop Exuperius.

'Even the Spains are on the brink of ruin and tremble daily as they recall the invasion of the Cimbri; and, while others suffer misfortunes once in actual fact, they suffer them continually in anticipation.'

In most cases there seems to have been little or no opposition apart from the protracted siege at Worms, which may have been undertaken by the Burgundians rather than Vandals, Suevi or Alans. We need to take the list of towns with a pinch of salt. We mostly have the writings of early Christian bishops to go on and the stories that survive often mix fact and legend. For example, Bishop Nicasius of Reims was allegedly killed by the Vandals and the city pillaged. However, another version of the story has Nicasius being killed by the Huns half a century later and yet another has him dying of smallpox. One thing is quite clear, which is that much of Gaul fell to the ravages of the barbarians in the months and years following the Rhine crossing.

So what were the Vandals seeking? The stories passed down to us imply wanton destruction, but rape, pillage and plunder could not have been their ultimate goal. Like migrants risking all to cross the Mediterranean today in order to get into Europe, they were desperate, impoverished and seeking a better life for themselves and their families. The very fact that they made their move in the depths of midwinter shows just how desperate they were. Each Roman town they took gave the invaders enough supplies for a brief period and then they would have to move on again, probably splitting up into small bands to range over a wide swath of territory to keep themselves fed and watered.

Later, in 451 when the Huns moved into Gaul, many of the Gallic towns closed their gates and resisted the onslaught. Then Aetius, the most important man in the Roman Empire at the time, saw Gaul as his power base. In 407 Stilicho cared little for Gaul, and the inhabitants felt cut off and excluded from Imperial power. As the Vandals approached their towns, the Romans inside the walls probably knew that the Imperial armies were unlikely to come to their rescue and so opening their gates may have been seen as the lesser of evils. Another stark difference between the Vandal and Hun invasions is that the latter crossed the Rhine in late April, when there would have been forage and supplies available in the countryside. Campaigning in winter made capturing towns with their stores a matter of life and death for the Vandals rather than simply an opportunity for loot.

An Unlikely Coalition

This is the story of the Vandals but they were only minority partners in a wider coalition of tribes at the time that they crossed the Rhine on the last day of 406. Of the Vandals themselves, we have already seen how the Asdings and Silings may have shared a common heritage and language but that they were two very separate groups with no sense of a common Vandal nation. If it had not been for the Alans, the Asding Vandals would probably have been wiped out by the Franks before the Rhine crossing. Later Roman chroniclers state that the Alans were the dominant partner in the coalition and it was only later that the Asdings came into ascendancy.

So who were the Alans?

Ammianus Marcellinus has this to say about them:

'The Alans (whose various people it is unnecessary now to enumerate) are divided between the two parts of the earth, but although widely separated from each other and roaming over vast tracts, as nomads do, yet in the course of time they have united under one name, and are, for short, all called Alans because of the similarity in their customs, their savage mode of life, and their weapons. For they have no huts and care nothing for using the ploughshare, but they live upon flesh and an abundance of milk, and dwell in wagons, which they cover with rounded canopies of bark and drive over the boundless wastes....

'Young men grow up in the habit of riding from their earliest boyhood and regard it as contemptible to go on foot; and by various forms of training they are all skilled warriors....

'Almost all the Alans are tall and handsome, their hair inclines to blond, by the ferocity of their glance they inspire dread, subdued though it is. They are light and active in the use of arms. In all respects they are somewhat like the Huns, but in their manner of life and their habits they are less savage.... Just as quiet and peaceful men find pleasure in rest, so the Alans delight in danger and warfare. There the man is judged happy who has sacrificed his life in battle, while those who grow old and depart from the world by a natural death they assail with bitter reproaches, as degenerate and cowardly; and there is nothing in which they take more pride than in killing any man whatever: as glorious spoils of the slain they tear off their heads, then strip off their skins and hang them upon their war-horses as trappings....

'They do not know the meaning of slavery, since all are born of noble blood, and moreover they choose as chiefs those men who are conspicuous for long experience as warriors.'

The Alans were a Sarmatian people whose language was Iranian rather than German. In stark contrast to the Germanic Vandals, they were nomads rather than settled farmers and they had developed a horse-based culture with warriors going into battle as a combination of light horse archers and more heavily-armed lancers. In the earlier years of the Roman Empire there are plentiful references to Sarmatians, with armoured horse archers being famously depicted on Trajan's column. In the fifth century, references to the Sarmatians tend to die off and the Alans show up everywhere. In all likelihood these are the same people – nomadic or semi-nomadic Iranians, some of whom occupied the Danube frontier in the late fourth century with others still out on the Eurasian steppes to the north of the Black Sea.

Although they were horse warriors, how many of the Alan horses could have survived a winter campaign with no forage? After spending early winter in the forested, hilly terrain of the east bank of the Rhine, it is quite likely that many or most of their horses would have perished or become food for the migrants. Even if some horses survived until Mainz was captured, it is unlikely that the town or others around would have had sufficient forage to supply a proper cavalry army. Therefore it is possible that in the early months of their campaign many Alans may have found themselves unexpectedly and uncomfortably on foot until they were able to round up more mounts from the countryside in the following spring and summer months.

When the coalition of Asdings, Silings, Alans and Suevi moved into Gaul in 406/7, it would seem that, like the Vandals, the Alans were themselves not a single cohesive entity. One group of Alans led by Goar broke off to find accommodation with the Imperial authorities and was given land to settle around Orléans as *foederati*. Others led by Respendial remained with the coalition which moved into Spain. Renatus Profuturus Frigeridus (quoted above) leads us to believe that this split amongst the Alans took place before the Rhine crossing.

The Suevi (also Suebi, or Sueves) were Germans whose homeland was between the upper Rhine and Danube. They were known to the early Imperial Romans and in their early days were famous for their hairstyle, which involved tying their long hair into a 'Swabian knot'. Those Suevi who joined up with the Vandals and Alans probably included remnants of the Marcomanni and Quadi, who disappear from the historical record at this time. They most likely also incorporated a number of Alamanni who were not content with staying put on the upper Rhine. As with most of the other migrants, some Suevi remained behind, lending their name to the region of Swabia in modern Germany, while others joined up with the Vandals. Like the Vandals they were primarily foot warriors who favoured hand-to-hand combat. Like the Vandals. Most were those who could afford it probably had horses but they would have been perfectly happy to dismount and fight on foot depending on the circumstances. Of course, with the problems of a winter campaign in early 407 most or all Suevi probably found themselves on foot.

Interestingly, Jerome does not mention the Suevi in his list of barbarians ravaging Gaul between 407 and 409. Instead he lists Quadi, Gepids,

Heruls, Saxons, Burgundians and Alamanni as the German tribes, in addition to the Vandals. Probably both the Vandal and Suevi migrants had picked up various elements of these peoples, with some Quadi in particular merging with the Suevi. For the most part the Gepids and Heruls, whose homeland was to the east of the Siling Vandals, stayed put and came under Hun overlordship but it is quite possible that some individuals joined up for the move west. Romans were notoriously casual in the names they gave the barbarian peoples beyond their frontiers, often preferring to give them ancient classical names in preference to more accurate nomenclature. So it was that the Huns, Goths and other eastern tribes were often referred to as 'Scythians'. As neither Gepids nor Heruls were classical barbarians, and their full impact on the Roman world came much later, it is certainly possible that in naming them Jerome was being accurate rather than showing his learning as a classical scholar.

Although most of the Burgundians and Alamanni remained on the Rhine rather than moving deeper into Gaul, it is quite likely that they took the opportunity of the general confusion to expand their territories to the west bank of the Rhine while some individuals joined up with the Suevi or Vandals. A few years later the Burgundians were on both sides of the river, with Worms their new power base. So if Worms fell after a siege then it is quite possible that this was the work of the Burgundians.

Jerome also says that Strasbourg fell to the barbarians. This town lies well to the south of Mainz and is opposite the Alamannic heartland which the Vandals seemed to have bypassed. The modern German-speaking inhabitants of Alsace, of which Strasbourg is the most important city, are the descendants of the ancient Alamanni who expanded their territory to include both sides of the upper Rhine including modern Alsace, Baden and German-speaking Switzerland. Today their local dialects are very similar, even if the Alsatians disparagingly refer to their cousins on the east bank of the Rhine as 'Swabians' despite the fact that Swabia-proper is further east. Even Gregory of Tours mixes them up in his brief description of the migration: 'The Vandals left their own country and burst into the Gauls under King Gunderic. And when the Gauls had been thoroughly laid waste they made for the Spains. The Suebi, that is, Alamanni, following them, seized Gallicia.' Possibly the Suevi crossed the Rhine further south near Strasbourg in league with their Alamannic cousins. Then the Alamanni, like the Burgundians at Worms, took advantage of the general confusion to take over Strasbourg and all of the Upper Rhine Valley, while the Suevi moved on.

The *Notitia Dignitatum* has a section for a *Comes Argentoratensis*, (Count of Strasbourg) but assigns him no troops, no officials and no towns. In the late-fourth century, Strasbourg and the upper Rhine into northern Switzerland was held by the *Legio VIII Augusta Pia Fedelis Constans*. This is probably the same unit named as the *Octavani* in the *Notitia Dignitatum* as part to the Italian field army. Maybe this was one of the units withdrawn by Stilicho to help him against Radagasius, leaving Strasbourg open for the Alamanni to take over. As Stilicho concluded a number of treaties with the Alamanni as well as the Franks to hold the Rhine for him, then it is also possible that Strasbourg was part of the deal. Either way it is more than likely that it was the Alamanni, not the the Vandals, who took the town in 407.

This leaves the Saxons. Here again Jerome is probably correct, although there is very little chance that Saxons formed part of the Vandal-Alan-Suevic coalition. Saxon raiders had been active in the North Sea and English Channel for several years before 407. The *Notitia Dignitatum* lists a command of the *Comes litoris Saxonici per Britanniam* (Count of the Saxon Shore of Britain) who defended the east coast of Britain against them. Several bands of sea-borne Saxons also penetrated the rivers of western France and there is some evidence to conclude that they also established settlements there. So as Jerome is describing the general state of Gaul rather than the specifics of the Vandal migration, his inclusion of Saxons makes some sense.

Going back to Jerome's list of barbarians, we have already seen how the Sarmatians and Alans were probably one and the same. This just leaves the 'Pannonians'. Pannonia is the region south of the Danube, before the bend, that includes parts of modern Austria, Hungary and Slovenia. This was Roman territory and, as Jerome's lamentation implies, some of the Roman inhabitants of this oft-ravaged region decided to throw in their lot with the migrants as a better option than remaining loyal to the Empire which had failed to protect them. Several years before the Rhine crossing, the Asding Vandals had crossed into Pannonia only to be driven back. Then in 405 Radagasius and his horde took the same route. The Pannonian peasants would have taken the brunt of these invasions and their livelihoods would have been destroyed.

As Roman power receded, the Imperial authorities were hard pressed to uphold the interests of the aristocracy, let alone protect the poorer elements of society. Throughout much of the fifth century there were endemic uprisings where groups of people took matters into their own hands to set up semi-independent enclaves which broke free from the heavy hand of taxation to basically rule themselves. These groups, called *Baccaudae* by Roman writers, were particularly active in Gaul and Spain in the mid-fifth century. Well before then, many Romans decided that they would be better off joining up with the invaders rather than passively accepting their depredations. When the Gothic refugees took up arms against Rome in 376 they were certainly joined by disaffected Romans, and the same was probably the case in 406/7.

Another explanation for Jerome's Pannonians could be that they were the survivors of the earlier Asding invasion of 401 who had been settled inside Roman territory as federates. This seems less likely. Most Germans who had been granted federate status tended to remain loyal to their new paymasters. After all, if they had found both land and a secure income why would they suddenly throw in their lot with new immigrants whose prospects were far from certain?

Coalitions survive when the mutual interests of the various partners are greater than the differences that separate them. We have seen this in modern politics where unlikely coalitions of political parties have held together against the odds. The Iranian Alans had nothing in common with the German Vandals and Suevi, yet although some bands split off, the coalition held together for many years after the Rhine crossing. Probably operating in dispersed groups, they survived a winter campaign by taking the towns of northern Gaul to supply themselves and, as they recouped their strength, they looked to find lands that they could call their own.

So how many barbarians crossed into Gaul in 406/7? Although we have no reliable figures, it is possible to make some deductions.

In 429 the Vandals probably crossed into Africa with 80,000 souls. This group included the survivors of the Silings and Alans who had been decimated in a devastating war with the Goths. After years of wandering, they would have lost many people along the way but also would have picked up others including disaffected Romans, not to mention more women and slaves. Furthermore, Goar's Alans had broken off from the main coalition and stayed behind in France. Taking all this into account, it is not unreasonable to assume that the Silings, Asdings and Alans may have had an average of 30,000 people each when they crossed into Gaul. The Silings probably the smallest group and the Alans the largest. The Suevi who stayed behind in Spain in 429 were concentrated in the region of one or two cities, which probably implies that they were not very numerous, probably no more than 20,000 people. Putting this all together gives us a rough estimate of just over 100,000 people, possibly up to a quarter of whom would have been fit males able to bear arms.

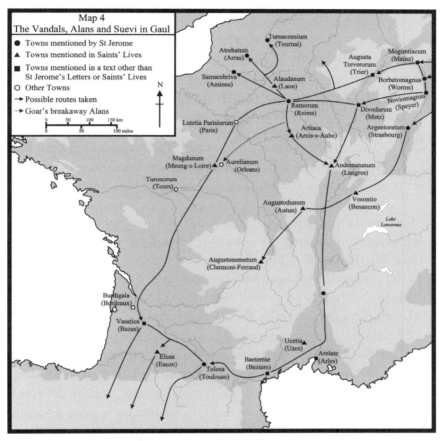

The Vandals, Alans and Suevi in Gaul AD 407-409 (after Heather). After they crossed the Rhine on 31 December 406 the majority of the Vandals, Alans and Suevi broke up into small bands and ranged widely over the country looking for supplies, while Goar's Alans broke away and were settled as Roman allies around Orléans. Constantine III bottled the others up in the north for a while after defeating some of them in battle. Roman civil wars gave the barbarians the opportunity to break out to the south, probably in late 408 or early 409. The routes shown on the map are conjectural, based on towns mentioned by various Roman writers.

Chapter 3

A Spanish Interlude

Constantine and the British Usurpations

Although Stilicho was otherwise occupied when the Vandals, Alans and Suevi moved into Gaul, the barbarians did not have everything their own way. Constantine crossed from Britain into Gaul at some point in 407 and Zosimus recounts his actions:

'The Vandals, uniting with the Alani and the Suevi, crossed [the Rhine], and plundered the countries beyond the Alps. Having there occasioned great slaughter they likewise became so formidable even to the armies in Britain, that they were compelled, through fear of their proceeding as far as that country, to choose several usurpers, as Marcus, Gratian, and after them Constantine.

'A furious engagement ensued between them in which the Romans gained the victory, and killed most of the barbarians. Yet by not pursuing those who fled, by which means they might have put to death every man, they gave them opportunity to rally, and by collecting an additional number of barbarians, to assume once more a fighting posture. For this cause, Constantine placed guards in these places, that those tribes should not have so free access into Gaul. He likewise secured the Rhine, which had been neglected since the time of the Emperor Julian.

'Having thus arranged affairs throughout all Gaul, he decorated his eldest son, Constans, with the habit of a Caesar, and sent him into Spain. For he wished to obtain the absolute sovereignty of that country, not only through the desire of enlarging his own dominions, but of diminishing the power of the relations of Honorius [who were of Spanish origin].'

The British field army at this time was not large, probably no more than 4-6,000 men. However, most of the Gallic Army, which was probably dispersed over several towns, came over to Constantine, although for a time Arles apparently remained loyal to Honorius and Stilicho. Constantine established a base at Orléans and if we are to accept Zosimus' account he engaged the Vandal coalition in battle, defeated them but failed to destroy them. Given a free hand, perhaps Constantine could have finished the job but he had to turn his attention south to deal with Sarus's army that Stilicho had sent against him.

After defeating Sarus, Constantine controlled most of Gaul. Zosimus' account leads us to believe that the Vandal coalition was licking its wounds in northern parts, leaving Constantine to turn his attention to Spain. Unfortunately for him, Gerontius, one of his generals whom he sent to Spain, took exception to the appointment of a rival and rose up in revolt. With Constantine's attention thus turned towards Spain and Italy, the Vandals were able to break loose from the frontier regions where they had been previously constrained. As Zosimus says:

'The greater part of his army being in Spain, the barbarians beyond the Rhine made such unbounded incursions over every province, as to reduce not only the Britons, but some of the Celtic nations also to the necessity of revolting from the Empire, and living no longer under the Roman laws but as they themselves pleased. The Britons therefore took up arms, and incurred many dangerous enterprises for their own protection, until they had freed their cities from the barbarians who besieged them. In a similar manner, the whole of Armorica, with other provinces of Gaul, delivered themselves by the same means; expelling the Roman magistrates or officers, and erecting a government, such as they pleased, of their own.'

Here we have a story not only of barbarian depredations but more interestingly a story of local inhabitants taking matters into their own hands in despair of official protection. The last remnants of the British field army left with Constantine and the inhabitants had no choice but to look to their own interests without any prospect of help from the authorities, whether these were in Italy or Gaul. Armorica (roughly modern Brittany) became a centre of the *Baccaudae* who defied Imperial control for decades. So with Constantine worried about Gerontius' usurpation in Spain and the threat from Stilicho in Italy, and the latter still focused on Alaric and his Goths, the Vandals, Suevi and Alans were presented with another opportunity.

Picking up Zosimus' narrative we learn that:

'Thus happened this revolt or defection of Britain and the Celtic nations, when Constantine usurped the Empire, by whose negligent government the barbarians were emboldened to commit such devastations. In the meantime, Alaric, finding that he could not procure a peace on the conditions which he proposed, nor had received any hostages, once more attacked Rome, and threatened to storm it if the citizens refused to join with him against the Emperor Honorius.'

Stilicho was executed by Honorius on 22 August 408. The convoluted politics which led to this are part of another story, but his fall from grace was no doubt tied to his failure to keep Gaul under Honorius' control. Following Stilicho's demise, Alaric's Goths were at the walls of Rome and the Vandals, Alans and Suevi crossed into Spain. So why did the Vandal coalition decide to move into Spain rather than trying to carve out a place for themselves in Gaul?

Most probably this was down to the actions of Constantine, combined with the ups and downs of Imperial politics. Constantine had the Gallic field army under his command, supplemented by the troops he had withdrawn from Britain as well as Frankish and Alammanic allies. In the immediate aftermath of Stilicho's execution there was no one of his stature to lead the army of Italy to defend Rome against Alaric, less alone intervene in the affairs of the West.

Therefore, as the first decade of the fifth century came to a close Italy was in chaos. Spain was tenuously held by the usurper Gerontius while Gaul, although devastated and with parts under the control of the *Baccaudae*, had the only leader capable of taking decisive action. Had they remained in Gaul, the Vandal coalition would have had to defeat Constantine. If Zosimus is correct then they had already had the worst of such an encounter.

So the Vandals and their allies moved south into the vacuum. If we accept Jerome's story (quoted in the previous chapter), they tried but failed to take Toulouse, thanks to the efforts of Bishop Exuperius who rallied the inhabitants. Ranging over the countryside and probably taking several routes, they would then have had to concentrate their forces to breach the Pyrenees. The passes were lightly held by troops locally engaged by Gerontius who seemed more interested in pillaging the country to supplement their wages than offering a defence to a determined enemy.

On the Road Again

The Spanish Bishop Hydatius says that the Vandals, Suevi and Alans crossed the passes into Spain in 409, 'on a Tuesday, some say 28 September, others say 13 October.' The passage of the mountain passes by tens of thousands of people with all their baggage and belongings would have taken quite some time. Possibly the period from 28 September to 13 October may have been the time it took for the migrants to move across the mountains and reach the yet unravaged country beyond. As it was highly unlikely that they were moving as a single body, most probably the first groups made it through the passes in late September with other groups following along behind.

By this point the coalition of Vandals, Alans and Suevi must have been a pretty hard-bitten lot. They had survived a winter campaign despite being burdened with families and baggage, and they had taken a good number of fortified Roman towns. They had survived a tough encounter with the Franks on the east bank of the Rhine and a defeat at the hands of Constantine's Roman Army. Yet against all the odds they had not only survived but had managed to stick together, despite the differences of language and culture. Amazingly, there seems to have been no single charismatic leader to hold the coalition together. After Godegisel's death in the battle with the Franks, his son Gunderic took over kingship of the Asdings, but there was no single leader. Each of the tribes had their own leaders and their coordinated movements must have been decided in council rather than being dictated by an overlord. Probably it was necessity which held them together for so long and although some, such as Goar's Alans, broke off to find their own way, the coalition held for several years, which is more than could be said for the Romans.

Picking up a coherent narrative from the tantalizing snippets various chroniclers have left us is not an easy task. This time the migration seems to have been planned rather than forced by necessity of starvation. Making their move in September/October would have given them time to gather in supplies from the southern Gallic countryside and then force the passes when the weather was still reasonable. Once across the mountains they would have needed to find somewhere suitable for winter quarters before spreading out over the countryside. Quite possibly they made towards Pompaelo and then may have rested there. Possibly some of them pushed on further towards Burgos, Leon and Zamora before stopping for the winter.

As soon as there was enough forage for their animals, in spring 410 the migrants apparently spread over the countryside. Hydatius is our primary source for the activities of the Vandals, Alans and Suevi at this time and he paints a pretty bleak picture. In a forewarning of the impending apocalypse he tells of the sack of Spain:

> 'While the barbarians ran wild through the Spanish provinces, and evil pestilence raged, the tyrannical tax collector plundered and the soldier used up the supplies stored in the cities. Terrible famine prowled, so that human beings were compelled by hunger to devour human flesh and mothers fed on the murdered and cooked bodies of those they had borne. Beasts, accustomed to the bodies of those slain by the sword, famine and plague, and fed by the bodies of whatever men they had killed, ran wild bringing death to the human race. And thus, with the four plagues of sword, famine, pestilence and beasts raging through the entire world, those things proclaimed by the Lord through his prophets were fulfilled.'

If the defence of Gaul had been problematic for Rome, then holding Spain in early 410 was even more so. The *Notitia Dignitatum* lists the *Comes Hispanias* (Count of Spain) controlling eleven *Auxilia Palatina* and five *Legiones Comitatenses*. At full strength this would have given him just over 10,000 men —far less than the Gallic field army which had not yet been able to destroy the invaders. Interestingly, there are no cavalry listed, and the *Comes Hispanias* does not have his own section in the *Notitia*. This has led some to conclude that the position was created later – around 420 when Hydatius mentions a *Comes Hispaniarum*. If this army was raised later then Gothic *foederati* could perhaps have supplied the cavalry contingent. The Spanish Army, however, does not include any *pseudocomitatenses* nor any units named after the Emperor Honorius, both of which might be expected of new units raised in 420. This leads me to believe that the Spanish field army was already in existence in 409, but we cannot know this for certain. It may be that Spain was undefended apart from around 4,000 *limitanei*. According to the *Notitia*, these were:

> *Septimae Geminae*, a legion at Legio (Léon)
> *Secundae Flaviae Pacatianae*, a cohort at Paetaonio (Rosinos de Vidriales, Zamora)
> *Secundae Gallicae*, a cohort at Cohortem Gallicam (unknown)
> *Lucensis*, a cohort at Lucus (Lugo)
> *Celtiberae*, a cohort at Brigantiae near Iuliobriga (Reinosa)
> *Primae Gallicae*, a cohort at Veleia (Iruña)

There was little chance that Rome's Spanish troops could do what their more numerous Gallic counterparts had so far failed to do. Furthermore, the Spanish Army had only just been won over to Constantine's cause before his general Gerontius rose up in revolt. Meanwhile, with Stilicho out of the way, Alaric sacked Rome and his Goths moved more or less at will through Italy. So as the Vandals, Suevi and Alans were making their acquaintance with the Spanish countryside, Gerontius decided to head off to Arles to confront Constantine and the Italian Army had its hands full with far more pressing problems. This left Spain to the barbarians.

Taking up the Plough

A life of perpetual plundering cannot be sustained. Eventually the potential sources dry up, and with famine raging through Spain this was what faced the Vandal coalition. So it was in 411 that they 'took up the plough', as Orosius recounts. This does not mean that they suddenly became farmers but rather settled down to rule over the local Hispano-Roman population. Hydatius says that the tribes divided up Spain by lot, with the Asdings getting eastern Gallaecia and the Suevi the western part (Roman Gallaecia being larger than modern Spanish Galicia). The

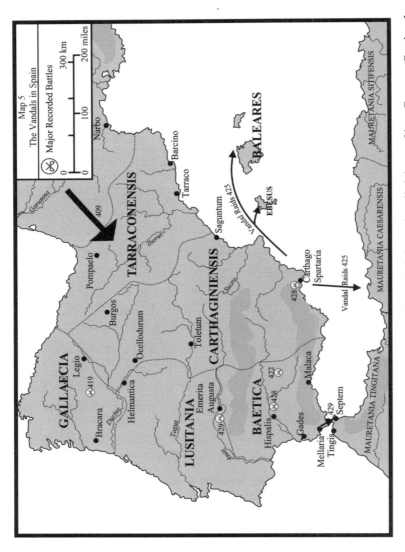

The Vandals in Spain AD 409–429. This map shows the administrative divisions of late Roman Spain along with the major towns and locations of those battles we know of which were fought by the Vandals. Unfortunately, we do not know the locations of the battles in which the Goths destroyed the Silings and decimated the Alans (416–418).

Silings took Baetica in the south while the Alans got Lusitania in the west and Carthaginiensis in the centre. The province of Tarraconensis in the north and north east remained under Gerontius' control. While the towns and cities of the interior opened their gates to their new overlords, many of the important ports such as Cartagena (*Carthago Spartaria*) stayed under Roman control.

Many modern historians have concluded that this division of Spain must have been part of a treaty with the Roman authorities which granted the barbarians these lands with federate status. However, none of the original sources give any sense of this settlement being part of a formal treaty and even if it had been, with whom could it have been made? Gerontius was the only Roman with any power in Spain and this was pretty tenuous. He was a usurper in conflict with another usurper (Constantine), and even if he had come to some accommodation with the barbarians, at best this could have been to simply abandon southern and western Spain to their depredations. Furthermore, there was no other external threat which the Romans may have wished to use the Vandals, Alans and Suevi to deal with. Nor was there any later occasion where these tribes acted on behalf of Rome. Indeed the opposite was true and in the years that followed the Romans did their damnedest to dislodge the invaders from their new homes.

So the barbarians probably decided the division of Spain amongst themselves, possibly alongside an understanding with Gerontius that he would not oppose them as long as they left Tarraconensis alone. The territorial division has also puzzled some historians in light of the later Asding ascendancy. They got one of the smallest and least fertile parts of the country, while the Alans got the best bits. This probably reflected both the relative strengths of each tribe in 411 and the parts of Spain they happened to be in at the time. Later, the cracks would begin to show in the coalition but in the immediate aftermath of the division each tribe settled down as overlords while the local population went about their business as usual, probably far less worried about who their new rulers were than the opportunity for a respite from their depredations.

The peace did not hold, and once again this was more due to Roman politics than any actions taken by the barbarians. In 411, Gerontius and his general Maximus left Spain for Gaul. They defeated Constantine's son Constans at Vienne and then moved down the Rhone to besiege the father at Arles. However, Gerontius' Spanish troops mutinied and the leaders fled back to Spain. Gerontius was eventually killed and Maximus ended his days holed up in the mountains. The Emperor Honorius had meanwhile appointed Constantius as Stilicho's successor. Alaric had died shortly after the Gothic sack of Rome and his successor was Ataulf. Again showing how the Romans saw usurpers as a greater threat than any group of barbarians, Constantius left Ataulf's Goths in Italy to move against Constantine at Arles. He was successful. Constantine was executed and after four years of semi-independence Gaul was brought back under Honorius' jurisdiction.

This just left the Imperial authorities with the knotty problem of Ataulf's Goths. What better solution could there be than to set them against the Vandals, Suevi and Alans in Spain? Probably initially on their own initiative and later with Roman encouragement, the Goths moved into southern Gaul. Together with some Burgundians and Goar's Alans, the Goths defeated yet another Roman usurper in 414 and then made their way via Narbonne into Tarraconensis to take Barcelona. None of this could have seriously worried Constantius nor the Emperor Honorius. Tarraconensis may have been free of barbarians before 414, but it had been Gerontius' base. Far better that the Goths should be there than rampaging through Italy or Gaul while the Imperial authorities tried to re-establish control over those provinces.

At this stage, however, the Goths were probably not yet operating as Roman surrogates and indeed there is some evidence that Ataulf and Constantius were unable to come to any formal agreement. Roman fleets blockaded the coasts, bringing famine. This forced the Goths to agree to a new accommodation with Ravenna (the West Roman capital at this time). Ataulf was murdered in September 415 and after a brief, bloody family struggle Wallia became the new king. He made his peace with Rome in exchange for supplies of grain, which probably came from the prosperous provinces of North Africa.

The End of the Coalition

For nearly five years the Vandals, Alans and Suevi had been able to enjoy the fruits of their conquests, but in 416 this came to an end as the Romans loosed the now compliant Goths onto them. Wallia's men captured a

Vandal king (probably a Siling) by the name of Fredibal and sent him as a captive to Ravenna. From 416 to 418, with Roman encouragement, the Goths waged war against the new barbarian overlords of Spain with devastating success. As Hydatius reports:

> 'The Siling Vandals in Baetica were wiped out by King Wallia. The Alans who were ruling over the Vandals and Suevi, suffered such heavy losses at the hands of the Goths that, after the death of their king, Addax [who had succeeded Respendial], the few survivors, with no thought to their won kingdom, placed themselves under the protection of Gunderic, the King of the Asding Vandals who had settled in Gallaecia.'

Until this point, Gunderic's Asdings had been one of the smaller partners in the coalition. Now, with the Silings wiped out and the Alans decimated, he absorbed the survivors to create a much more powerful group which had so far managed to avoid the Gothic attacks. Quite probably it had been a blessing in disguise when the Asdings ended up with the poorer territories of Spain when the coalition divided up the country. Much later the Asding King Huneric is recorded as styling himself as *Rex Vandalorum et Alanorum* but such a title may well have been assumed shortly after the defeat of the Alans at the hands of the Goths and their absorption by the Asdings. From 418 there was only one group of Vandals and the term 'Asding' came to be used to describe the royal line rather than a single Vandal clan.

Finally, after more than a decade of holding together against all odds, the coalition broke apart in the aftermath of the disastrous war with Wallia's Goths. Conflict broke out between the Vandals and Suevi, and although we do not know the cause it was most likely due to pressure on the Vandals. Whether due to fate or design, the Asdings had drawn the short straw in the divvying up of lots for territory in 411. Wallia had destroyed the Silings and driven the Alans out of their choice holdings. No doubt once the Goths had been withdrawn to Gaul and were given Aquitaine as a reward for their efforts, Baetica, Lusitania and Carthaginiensis reverted back to Roman control. The Asdings were bottled up in eastern Gallaecia and if this may have been just enough for them on their own, they now had to absorb the Alan and Siling refugees who had been displaced by the Goths.

Despite their modern reputation as fearsome warriors, the Vandals did not have a very good military track record when it came to pitched battle. In 401 the first Vandal raiders had been defeated by Stilicho. Then in 405 they were on the brink of defeat at the hands of the Franks, only to be rescued by the Alans in the nick of time. When Constantine took to the field against them he too won his battle, even if he failed to destroy them. Then, finally, the Silings were destroyed by Wallia's Goths. With a near perfect string of military defeats, how was it that they had survived so far and how was it that they had managed to cut a swathe through Gaul and Spain? The answer to this probably lies in the long history of the trouble organized military forces have always had in bringing even small bands of determined guerrillas to heel. There were very few technological differences between the Romans, Goths or Vandals. What the Romans excelled in, when they were not fighting amongst themselves, was organization and structure.

A number of contemporary historians are fairly scathing about the Vandals' military abilities. The Spanish chronicler Orosius describes them as 'unwarlike, avaricious, perfidious and crafty'. The Gallo-Roman writer Salvian says: 'God, by handing over the Spanish nation to the Vandals for punishment, showed in a double degree his hatred of the sins of the flesh, since the Spaniards were conspicuous for their immorality and the Vandals for their chastity, while the latter were the weakest of all the barbarian tribes.'

The Goths had time to learn and develop more cohesive military structures in the many years they had been a pseudo-Roman Army in the aftermath of their victory at Adrianople in 378, but the Vandals had not. They may have been tough – indeed they must have been to survive all they had been through. However, they never had time to develop the command and control structures needed for success in pitched battle. They had been more or less constantly on the move since 400 and were more used to operating in small dispersed bands than they were marshalling the large coherent force needed for victory in formal battle.

The Suevi were in a similar situation and therefore Gunderic's Vandals finally won success on the field against their former allies. They defeated King Hermanric's Suevi, driving them into the mountains of Asturias. Success was short-lived. Castinus, the new Roman governor of Spain, moved against the Vandals in 419 and seemed to get the better of an encounter with a group of them near Hydatius' home town of Braga in western Gallaecia. This won Castinus the high office of *Comes Domesticorum* (Count of the Imperial Guard), although the victory seems to have been more symbolic rather than one which greatly diminished Vandal strength. Indeed, the outcome seems to have been to cause the Vandals to leave Gallaecia and push south to occupy the former Siling territories of Baetica in southern Spain.

The Romans, however, did not let up the pressure. In 422 they launched a seaborne invasion against Baetica, together with Gothic allies. Once again the Vandals were saved by internal Roman politics, as Hydatius tells us:

'At this time an army was sent to Spain against the Vandals with Castinus as commander. By an unsuitable and unjust order he excluded Boniface, a man quite well known for military skill, from partnership in his expedition. As a result Boniface judged Castinus as dangerous to himself and unworthy to be followed since he [Boniface] found him [Castinus] to be quarrelsome and proud. So Boniface rushed quickly to Portus and thence to Africa. And this was the beginning of many troubles for the state.'

We shall hear more of Boniface and the 'troubles for the state' in the following chapter.

Despite Boniface's defection, Castinus had some initial success, bottling up the Vandals in an unnamed city. His Gothic allies deserted when he attempted an assault, and when Castinus unwisely risked open battle he was defeated. According to Salvian, the Vandals carried a bible as a standard in front of them and, whether or not they benefitted from divine intervention, they won the second battle in their history and their first against Romans. They drove the surviving Romans and Goths back to Tarraconensis.

At this point it is worth a brief pause from the narrative to again look at the question of religion. As mentioned in Chapter 1, some early chroniclers say that the Vandals were still heathens when they crossed the Rhine and only converted later. Hydatius says that Geiseric, who succeeded Gunderic as king in 428, was originally Catholic and only later became an Arian. The Vandal Arian faith had a large impact on their history in Africa and it is pretty clear that the Vandals were Arian Christians by the time they got there. It may be that the Suevi and Alans were later converts, but if the Vandals had only converted on arrival in Spain then they would almost certainly have become Catholics, as the only other Arians around at that time were their bitter enemies, the Goths. Far more likely, therefore, that they had come under the influence of Ulfilas when they were still living in Germania in the fourth century. Any religious fervour they showed at the battle with Castinus' Romans was probably of the Arian sort and had already become part of their distinct identity which set them apart from the Catholic Romans. If it is indeed true that the Vandals carried a bible or some other religious icon as a standard against the Romans, then it is far more likely to have been something that marked them in opposition to their enemies rather than demonstrating a shared faith.

After the failed Roman invasion of Baetica, the Vandals were given another interlude as the Western Empire was thrown into upheaval. The Emperor Honorius died on 27 August 423 and once again Romans fell out amongst themselves. In the chaos that followed, Spain was left alone and the Vandals used the time to expand their territory. In 425 they raided the Balearic Isles and Mauretania on the African coast. This is the first time the people who originated from the centre of Europe, about as far away from the sea as is possible, are recorded using ships. It would not be the last time. No doubt, following the abortive Roman campaign of 422, the Vandals had been able to seize the port cities, such as Cartagena, that had previously been closed to them. It is impossible that the Vandals had suddenly become master seafarers but it would have been no great difficulty to commandeer boats or commission others to be built. These would not have been warships, but rather vessels that could transport Vandal warriors to the undefended coastal regions which previously would have been difficult or impossible to reach.

At this point one might think that the Vandals would have been reasonably content with their place in the sun. However, Spain was no longer the unplundered land that had beckoned them in 409. With only very brief interludes of peace, it had been fought over almost continually for the last two decades. If Hydatius' account is anything to go on – and he should know as he lived through those times – it had become a place of devastation, famine and pestilence. Furthermore, despite Rome's new internal troubles, there was no indication than the Imperial authorities would leave the Vandals alone in Spain once they had settled their own internal disputes.

Having gained access to the sea and by raiding the North African coast, the Vandals would have become aware that there were new, fruitful and unplundered lands apparently ripe for the taking. As Victor of Vita recounted in 484:

'Finding a province [Africa] which was at peace and enjoying quiet, the whole land beautiful and flowering on all sides, they [the Vandals] set to work on it with their wicked forces, laying it waste by devastation and bringing everything to ruin with fire and murders.'

Once again, Roman politics provided the opportunity and the impetus to set the Vandal wanderers on the move. This time the changes in the Roman regime were also mirrored by political changes amongst the Vandals.

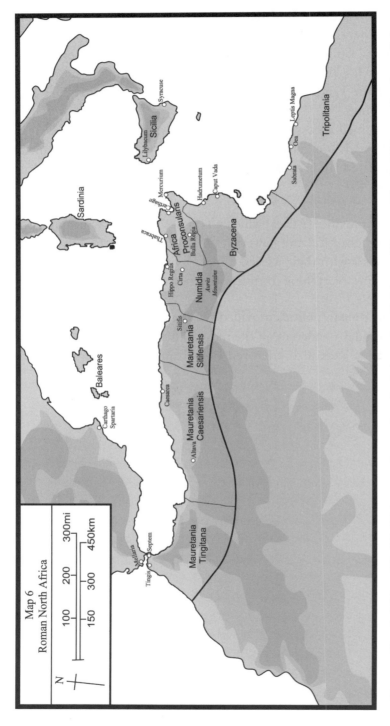

Roman North Africa AD 429. This map shows the administrative divisions of Roman North Africa at the time of the Vandal invasion. The Vandals probably crossed from Mellaria to Septem and then made their way along the coast to reach Hippo Regius in 430. They took Carthage in October 439. In later years, the Moors used the Aurès Mountains as a base from which they raided Vandal territory.

Chapter 4

Into Africa

A Possible Invitation

We have to turn again to Roman politics to understand why the Vandals decided to leave the land they had fought tooth and nail over to hold against all comers for the past two decades. By this time many of the young warriors filling the Vandal ranks had been born inside the Roman Empire and they had only folk tales to remind them of their forefathers' ancestral home in the forests of Germania. Yet, unlike the Franks, Alamanni, Burgundians or Goths they had not received any formal settlement with Rome and they remained unwelcome foreigners in the land to which they had been born.

After Honorius' death, the infant Valentinian III ascended to the Western throne at Ravenna, with his mother Galla Placidia the power behind it. She was propped up by the Eastern Empire but more importantly by three powerful warlords: Aeitus, Felix and Boniface. Each of these men vied to become the pre-eminent general who would rule the Western Empire in all but name. After some initial struggles, Aeitus, backed up by Huns, was given command of the Gallic field army. Felix got the Italian army while Boniface, the same man who had fallen out with Castinus in his campaign against the Vandals in 422, became the Count of Africa.

Galla Placidia did her best to keep a balance between these powerful warlords but conflict was inevitable. In 427, Boniface was accused of disloyalty by Felix and was ordered to return to Italy. When Boniface refused, Ravenna tried to bring him back by force, without much success.

'By the decision of Felix, war in the public name was declared on Boniface, whose power and glory were growing in Africa, because he refused to return to Italy. The war was prosecuted by Mavortius, Gallio and Sanoex. By the treason of the last of these, Mavortius and

Gallio were killed while they were besieging Boniface, and Mavortius himself was soon killed by Boniface when his deceit was uncovered.' (Prosper of Aquitaine)

In the midst of these Imperial struggles, the Vandals saw their chance. They may even have been invited into Africa by Boniface when his position was under threat from Felix and Aetius. Even if the invitation was not so direct, then he may well have let it be known that he was in the market for mercenaries to prop up his position in Africa.

According to Procopius, writing in the sixth century, Boniface sent an embassy to the Vandals just after Gunderic's death (although he confuses Gunderic with Godegisel):

'Boniface accordingly sent to Spain those who were his most intimate friends and gained the adherence of the sons of Godigiselus on terms of complete equality. It being agreed that each one of the three, holding a third part of Libya, should come to rule over his own subjects but if a foe should come against any one of them to make war that they should in common ward off the aggressors. On the basis of this agreement the Vandals crossed the straits of Gadira [Gibraltar] and came into Libya.'

Historians have debated the validity of Procopius' account for centuries. Some dismiss the idea that the Vandals were invited into Africa entirely, while others hedge their bets. However, Procopius is not the only source. Jordanes gives a similar account: 'Geiseric, King of the Vandals, had already been invited into Africa by Boniface, who had fallen into a dispute with the Emperor Valentinian and was able to obtain revenge only by injuring the Empire. So he invited them urgently and brought them across the narrow strait known as the Strait of Gades, scarcely seven miles wide, which divides Africa from Spain and unites the mouth of the Tyrrhenian Sea with the waters of Ocean.'

Finally we have this tantalizing snippet from Prosper as he continues his account of the conflict between Boniface and Felix (quoted above):

'After that [Boniface's defeat of Felix's generals] access to the sea was gained by peoples who were previously unaccustomed with the use of ships, when they were called on to help the rivals. The conduct of the war begun against Boniface was transferred to Count Sigisvult.'

Prosper's next entry simply reads: 'The Vandal people crossed from Spain to Africa.'

Sigisvult was a Goth and so Prosper's passage could easily mean that Goths were transported by sea to aid Felix, but it more likely means that the Vandals were called in by Boniface, particularly in light of the follow-on entry. As Prosper uses the plural he could well be reporting that barbarians were called in to support both factions.

The main argument against Boniface's invitation is that a year later he was leading the defence of Africa against them. However, by 429 he had been reconciled with Galla Placidia. By then, if he had previously sought Vandal help, it would have been too late for him to say that he no longer needed it even if he had 'repented of his act', as Procopius says.

Despite the tendency of many modern historians to try to rehabilitate Boniface's reputation, for me the stories ring true. Although they had survived against all odds for two decades, the one thing the Vandals had failed to achieve was a permanent accommodation within the Roman Empire where they could be left alone to enjoy the fruits of their victory rather than having to constantly look over their shoulders to the next attack.

In 428/29, the situation in Spain was perhaps not great but the Vandals did not have an immediate threat to their position. With Boniface, Felix and Aetius facing each other off in Africa, Italy and Gaul, then the Vandals could perhaps have anticipated a few uninterrupted years of peace in Spain, just as the Suevi did, who decided to remain behind. Furthermore, with Aetius trying to build a power base in Gaul, the Goths' attention was drawn towards the north and west rather than to Spain. In order to spark off yet another migration, the motivation had to be more than a yet unplundered province across the Straits of Gibraltar. The one thing that the Vandals lacked and which they needed more than anything was legitimacy. In the end they never really got it because they backed the losing side. However, an offer of land in return for backing one or another of the rival Roman factions seems to me to be the only reasonable explanation for the Vandals picking up sticks once again and heading off into a new and uncertain future.

In all likelihood there was no formal treaty, just as there had been none in 406 if Stilicho's ambassadors had been speaking smooth words around the council fires back then, nor in 411 when Gerontius' men no doubt gave assurances they could never hope to keep. In all likelihood the Vandals would have received embassies from all the competing Roman generals, if only to sound them out. Possibly, if Gunderic had remained king he would have thought twice about jumping on empty promises offered by Roman diplomats from yet another faction. But Gunderic died in 428 and his half-brother Geiseric took over.

New King of a New Nation

Although Geiseric was made King of the Vandals and Alans over Gunderic's two young sons, there is no evidence to suggest that this was a palace coup. Later, when Geiseric's power was greater, he still had to defer at times to the wishes of the other powerful Vandal leaders. Quite probably he was elected to the kingship in the old fashioned Germanic way by acclamation of the nobles. On taking the leadership he had the backing of the most important warriors, who would not have wanted to confer kingship on a minor. Later, however, Geiseric did away with the two inconvenient princes to secure the succession for his own son.

Geiseric (also variously spelled Gaiseric, Gizeric and Genseric) was Gunderic's half-brother, son of Godegisel and a Roman concubine. As he lived until 477 he must have been a fairly young man in 428 and was probably only an infant when the Vandals crossed the Rhine with his brother already king. If the story of his later conversion to Arianism is true, it may be that his mother had brought him up as a Catholic but that he adopted the Arian religion of his people as an adult.

Writing a century later, Jordanes paints a brief pen picture of the man:

'Geiseric, still famous in the City for the disaster of the Romans, was a man of moderate height and lame in consequence of a fall from his horse. He was a man of deep thought and few words, holding luxury in disdain, furious in his anger, greedy for gain, shrewd in winning over the barbarians and skilled in sowing the seeds of dissension to arouse enmity. Such was he who, as we have said, came at the solicitous invitation of Boniface to the country of Africa. There he reigned for a long time, receiving authority, as they say, from God Himself.'

Procopius says that: 'Geiseric had been excellently trained in warfare and was the cleverest of all men.'

Geiseric would have wanted to make a mark to differentiate him from his brother who had led the Asdings from the Rhine to the Mediterranean. Just as a politician being elected today needs to offer the people a vision of a new and better future, the recently-appointed king of the remaining Vandals and Alans had to do much the same thing. If he had some form of agreement with Boniface, no matter how vague, it would have been something he could have held up to his people of a promise of a better life under a new regime. So it was in May 429 Geiseric gathered his people at Mellaria (modern Tarifa, near Gibraltar) to make the crossing into Africa.

Who were these people, whom from this point onwards I will generically refer to as 'Vandals'? Clearly many were the descendants and survivors of the Asdings, Silings and Alans who had moved into Spain in 411. Yet everyone over the age of 23 had been born inside the Roman Empire and many of these, like Geiseric himself, to Roman mothers. On the long road to the south coast of Spain they had suffered many casualties, with the Silings being more or less wiped out and the Alans decimated. The survivors of both these previously separate groups were now integrated under Asding leadership. Escaped slaves, brigands and deserters from various Roman armies no doubt also swelled their ranks, as did a band of Goths who had ended up on the wrong end of a Gothic power struggle, remaining in Spain when their compatriots moved back to Aquitaine. Although the spilt with the Suevi had been violent, there may well have been some Suevi who threw their lot in with the Vandals. A tombstone of a Suevic woman, Ermengon, wife of Ingomar, who died in 474 was found at Hippo Regius (Annaba in modern Algeria), giving some evidence that this may have been the case.

So they were a pretty mixed bunch. The Asdings, Silings, Suevi and Goths would all originally have had a Germanic mother tongue (although probably 'father tongue' would be a more accurate term) but the Alans spoke an entirely different language and also had very different customs. How these various peoples managed to integrate can only be guessed at, as they left little or no archaeological or literary traces behind. Later mosaics from North Africa show that they had adopted Roman dress but that their horses had large cruciform *tagma* brands often associated with Sarmatian peoples such as the Alans. Although individual families probably retained their own original dialects for a generation or two, Latin would have been the only practical language of communication across groups. Increasingly, the Vandals would have adopted customs and practices that suited their current situation rather than clinging on to what had been appropriate for their Alan and German forefathers beyond the Rhine and Danube. What held them together and set them apart was recognition of the Asding dynasty as *Reges Vandalorum et Alanorum* and a fierce adherence to the Arian form of Christianity.

Across the Sea

Before actually moving into Africa, there was one last Spanish drama to play out. Hydatius reports that on learning that the Suevi, under their new King Heremigarius, were plundering the nearby provinces, Geiseric turned back inland to attack them:

> 'And so Geiseric returned with some of his men and pursued the looter into Lusitania. Heremigarius had previously inflicted harm on Emerita Augusta [Mérida] and the blessed martyr Eulalia; and not far from that city, after the accursed among his company had been killed by Geiseric ... he [Heremigarius] was cast down into the River Ana by the arm of God and died. After Heremigarius had thus been destroyed, Geiseric sailed away as he had begun to do so.'

It seems rather unlikely that once in the throes of his amphibious preparations Geiseric would have decided to march inland to the further reaches of his domains to defend territory he had already decided to abandon. More likely this engagement took place before the decision to move into Africa had been taken. Perhaps, although victorious, this new bout of Suevic aggression helped to convince any waverers amongst the Vandal nobles that leaving Spain was the best plan.

The number of 80,000 Vandals is generally accepted as a reliable figure for the entire Vandal nation that moved into Africa. Procopius says that there were 80,000 warriors, but even he doubts they could have had that many fighting men:

'The Vandals and the Alans he [Geiseric] arranged in companies, appointing over them no less than 80 leaders whom he called Chillarchs (leaders of 1,000), making it appear that his host of fighting men in active service amounted to 80,000. And yet the number of the Vandals and Alans was said in former times to amount to no more than 50,000.'

Victor of Vita tells us that before embarking, Geiseric carried out a full enumeration of the entire population, presumably so that he could organize transport and supplies. This census counted all the males 'old men, young men and children, slaves and masters'. Although Victor seems to discount the female population, a figure of 80,000 souls giving a potential fighting force of 15-20,000 men seems reasonable. An average of 20,000 men seems to be the size of most large Roman era armies and was probably the most that could be sustained on campaign without a Herculean effort. It equates to the two-legion Consular armies of the Republic as well as the field armies of the later Empire. With a highly-organized commissariat and with pre-positioning supplies, the Romans could temporarily combine larger numbers for a limited period for a specific campaign. Neither the Vandals nor any other barbarian force could possibly manage to do this. If the Vandals could muster close to 20,000 warriors, then it would have put them on a par with the larger Roman field forces sent against them while seriously outnumbering the dispersed garrisons of *limitanei*.

Moving an entire population of 80,000 people would have been an incredibly difficult and dangerous undertaking. First there was the matter of transport. It has been suggested by some historians that the Vandals could have sailed from Tarifa along the coast of Africa to land somewhere in modern Algeria. With the number of people, animals and supplies they had to carry, this would have been an impossible task. From Procopius we learn that the ships of the East Roman invasion fleet of 533 could each carry about seventy men plus horses and supplies. There is no chance that Geiseric could have had a fleet of over 1,000 ships capable of a long voyage. Therefore it is certain that they took the short route across the Straits of Gibraltar, probably heading for Septem (modern Ceuta).

This amphibious operation probably resembled something like the British retreat from Dunkirk in 1940, with an unlikely conglomeration of boats ferrying groups of people, animals and supplies over a protracted period. Unlike the British, however, there is no indication that the Vandals had any enemy action to contend with. *Mauretania Tingitana*, the name of the province which is now northern Morocco, was on the fringes of the Roman world and it was only lightly held by eight dispersed detachments of *limitanei* and a small field force of four infantry and three cavalry units. These troops would have been more used to regulating trade and keeping order than standing up to a major invasion. Two of the Count of Tingitania's infantry units were *Legiones Comitatenses*, which probably had a paper strength of 1,000 men each. The other two were Moorish *Auxilia Palatina*, probably up to 500 men each, with the same number for each of the three cavalry units. In the unlikely event that these units were at full strength, then the Count had at most 4,500 field army troops under his command and probably far less. Furthermore, if there was any confusion over the status of the Vandals resulting from the politicking of Boniface, Felix and Aeitus it would have taken a very brave man to make the unilateral decision to resist the Vandals without waiting for further instructions and reinforcements.

The ferrying back and forth between Spain and Africa must have gone on for weeks or even months. Many of the transports would have been relatively small craft commandeered from local fishermen and merchants rather than purpose-built transports. Ferrying 80,000 people would have been a monumental undertaking, but adding in all the wagons, supplies and livestock needed to support the Vandals would have made it even more difficult. No doubt Geiseric fully expected to be able to commandeer supplies and transport once he got to the other side, but keeping 80,000 people fed while they had to remain in a relatively small area as the amphibious operation was still going on would have been a Herculean task.

This brings us to the matter of horses and the nature of the Vandal army at this point in their history. Transporting horses by sea is far from impossible. In 533, Belisarius transported several thousand cavalrymen from Constantinople to Africa but this would have been done in purpose-built ships, few of which were likely to have been in Vandal possession in 429. By 533, the Vandal army was an entirely mounted force and seems to have lost the art of fighting on foot. If this was already the case in 429, then Geiseric would have had to transport around 20,000 cavalry mounts in addition to 80,000 people and all the livestock needed to haul the baggage wagons.

We have already seen how the Alans had a tradition of mounted warfare but that most of the Vandals probably fought on foot in their early days. Any ability to keep a decent stock of cavalry mounts probably took a beating in the winter of 406/7, and while the Vandals and Alans would no doubt have been able to round up replacement horses from the countryside these would have been a motley collection of nags rather than fine cavalry chargers. In Spain they may have had time to build up a decent horse herd, and certainly the Alans would have done their best to do so. They would, however, have been dependent on an initial breeding stock and the Roman field army in Spain was an entirely infantry force. Therefore, the number of good replacement war horses available to them would have been quite limited.

My conclusion is that a large proportion of the Vandal warriors probably crossed the Straits of Gibraltar without mounts. It was only later, once they had settled down in North Africa, that they were able to raise and maintain the number of trained horses needed to fight exclusively on horseback.

Across the Desert

Despite monumental difficulties the Vandals made it into Africa, apparently without serious mishap. However, their challenge was not yet over. In order to reach the more prosperous eastern provinces of Roman Africa, which were their target, they had a march of nearly 2,000km ahead of them.

With thousands of migrants risking their lives to cross in rickety boats from Africa to Europe in modern times, it is perhaps difficult for us to understand how the traffic was in the other direction a millennia and a half ago.

Back in the fifth century, Africa was the most prosperous region of the West Roman Empire. For years African agricultural surpluses were exported to Europe, and in particular fed the population of the city of Rome. In the nineteenth century, many historians concluded that the climate must have been different, but modern investigations do not bear this out. The climate was more or less as it is now, although there would have been more trees and therefore less desertification. The relatively fertile coastal strip along the Mediterranean has always been able to produce grain, olives, fruit and pasture. The big advantage Africa had before the arrival of the Vandals was that it had enjoyed many centuries of relative peace and stability since the end of the Punic and Numidian Wars.

While Italy, Gaul, Britain, and later Spain, endured the ravages of civil wars and barbarian invasions, Africa was largely spared. There had been a few conflicts with the Moors and the odd usurpation, but recent archeological discoveries show that the scattered Roman fortresses along the long desert frontier were more like customs posts than the defensive bastions of the French Foreign Legion which took their place in modern times.

Tingitana (modern northern Morocco), where the Vandals landed, was not the best part of Africa back then. Although fertile, it was on the very edge of civilization and was actually considered part of Spain rather than Africa. Had they been only seeking a safe haven to settle, then perhaps they could have done worse than to take it for themselves, but the Vandals were playing for higher stakes and the rich easterly provinces of Numidia, Byzacena and Africa Proconsularis drew them onwards. If there had been an earlier understanding with Boniface, these were the lands he controlled and perhaps his ambassadors had led the Vandals to believe that they could legally have a third of it for themselves. These regions contained the great cities of Hippo Regius (Annaba in modern Algeria) and Carthage (now a suburb of Tunis), not to mention many smaller towns and hugely prosperous farming estates. To get there, the Vandals had to cross 250km of desert and then move through the relatively poor province of Mauretania Caesariensis. So that is precisely what what they did.

We know very little about their route or what happened along the way, but it must have been a very arduous journey, with many people and animals failing to make it to the end. They no doubt followed the coastal road and may well have been supported by supply ships following along out to sea, but there is no hard evidence to prove this one way or another. The only clue comes from Altava (Ouloud Mimoun in modern Algeria),

500km east of where the Vandals first landed. Here an inscription records the death of a provincial official who died 'by barbarian sword' in late summer 429 – four months after the start of this last Vandal migration.

The tale of the Vandal trek across Africa is recounted in lurid detail by Victor of Vita (Victor Vitensis), a fifth century African bishop, in his not so subtlety named book *History of the Persecutions of the African Provinces at the time of the Vandal Kings*. He seems to almost relish the tales of death, mayhem and destruction as the Vandals laid waste to the countryside, despoiling virgins and torturing pious Catholic bishops: 'So it was that no place remained safe from being contaminated by them as they raged with great cruelty, unchanging and relentless.'

As in Gaul, the Vandals seem to have taken the cities and towns of Mauretania Caesariensis with relative ease. After pausing briefly to replenish supplies and wreak a little havoc on the Catholic population, the Vandals continued to push relentlessly eastward.

In their terror at the Vandal advance, the good bishops of Africa wrote to Saint Augustine in Hippo Regius asking him if it were permissible to flee and leave their flocks to their fate or if they were expected to 'reap the fruit of martyrdom'. When Augustine helpfully told them; 'Christ laid down His life for us: and we ought to lay down our lives for the brethren,' Bishop Honoratus of Thiabe took issue: 'I do not see what good we can do to ourselves or to the people by continuing to remain in the churches, except to see before our eyes men slain, women outraged, churches burned, ourselves expiring amid torments applied in order to extort from us what we do not possess?'

If the Vandal depredations were indeed as horrific as the early church fathers say they were, how was it that the towns along the way fell so easily? Supplies would have been the Vandals' most important goal. While they could ravage the countryside more or less at will, their main purpose in capturing a town would have been to gain access to the grain stores. The Vandals had neither the time nor the inclination to conduct a protracted siege before they reached the more prosperous provinces further on. Therefore, they would have depended on the inhabitants throwing their gates open to them or at least not offering a stubborn resistance. If the defenders knew that the result of surrender would be torture, death and violent destruction, they would have held out at all costs. Even if the dispersed detachments of *limitanei* under the Duke of Mauretania Caesariensis' command were not top notch troops, any sort of determined resistance would have inflicted unacceptable delays on the Vandal advance. In another of Victor's grisly accounts he says that the Vandals piled bodies against the walls to force surrender through fear of disease – a most unlikely tactic!

Of course not all towns would have had good walls, and those could have been taken by storm. It is also likely that the Vandal depredations hit the Catholic clergy and the nobility much harder than the poor, and that the horror expressed in contemporary writings reflect this. Throwing open the gates, therefore, may not have necessarily led to a general massacre. Various heretical Christian sects had sprung up in North Africa, and amongst them were the *Agonistici*, who were opposed to slavery and private property. They saw themselves as fighters for Christ and deliberately sought martyrdom, often through committing violent acts like modern suicide bombers. Men such as these would probably have had a very different take on the Vandals, as would the vast armies of slaves and poor farmers who toiled on the large estates to feed the mob in Rome. Unfortunately, their views and those of the Vandals themselves have gone unrecorded.

That said, the real horror felt by the Catholic clergy who wrote about the Vandal invasion should not be dismissed. The impact of the swift and unexpected advance of the Vandals and their vigorous persecution of those who held different religious views must have been similar to the impact felt today by many people in Syria and Iraq as their homelands are overrun by the so-called Islamic State.

Showdown with Boniface

By early 430 the Vandals had reached Numidia and Africa Proconsularis. Hippo Regius held against them, so many of the Vandals spread out over the provinces, probably in small groups of mounted warriors, now well supplied with horses rounded up from countryside.

An attempt to surprise the garrison and take Carthage in a *coup de main* failed and then Vandal bands pulled back to concentrate near Hippo Regius as the Romans were on the move. Whether or not Boniface's ambassadors had egged the Vandals on when he was in conflict with

Ravenna, Boniface certainly did not want them on his patch now that he was back in Galla Placidia's good books. After marshalling his forces, he marched on Hippo Regius to stop the Vandal advance.

The Vandals were at this time in the prosperous heartland of Roman Africa, which was also the best defended. As Count of Africa, Boniface had a good-sized field army under his command in addition to his sixteen detachments of *limitanei*. Again falling back on the *Notitia Dignitatum*, the theoretical order of battle for the African field army included the following units:

Senior Palatine Legions (*legiones palatinae*). The most best regular heavy infantry – probably around 1,000 men at full strength:

Armigeri Propugnatores Seniores
Armigeri Propugnatores Iuniores
Secundani Italiciani
Cimbriani

Palatine Auxiliaries (*auxilia platinae*). Elite infantry capable of mobile operations as well as standing firm in line of battle – probably about 500 men at full strength:

Celtae Iuniores

Legions of the Comitatus (*legiones comitatenses*). Good line heavy infantry – probably around 1,000 men at full strength:

Prima Flavia Pacis
Secunda Flavia Virtutis
Tertiani (Tertia Flavia Salutis)
Constantiniani (Secunda Flavia Constantiniana)
Constantici (Flavia Victrix Constantina)
Tertio Augustani
Fortenses

Cavalry of the Comitatus (*vexillationes comitatenses*). Good line cavalry - probably around 500 men each at full strength:

Equites Stablesiani Italiciani (heavy cavalry)
Equites Scutarii Seniores (heavy cavalry)
Equites Stablesiani Africani (heavy cavalry)
Equites Marcomanni (heavy cavalry)
Equites Armigeri Seniores (heavy cavalry)
Equites Sagittarii Clibanarii (armoured horse archers)
Equites Sagittarii Parthi Seniores (horse archers)
Equites Cetrati Seniores (possibly light cavalry)
Equites Primo Sagittarii (horse archers)
Equites Secundo Sagittarii (horse archers)
Equites Tertio Sagittarii (horse archers)
Equites Quarto Sagittarii (horse archers)
Equites Sagittarii Parthi Iuniores (horse archers)
Equites Cetrati Iuniores (possibly light cavalry)
Equites Promoti Iuniores (heavy cavalry)
Equites Sagittarii Iuniores (horse archers)
Equites Honoriani Iuniores (heavy cavalry)
Equites Secundi Scutarii Iuniores (heavy cavalry)
Equites Armigeri Iuniores (heavy cavalry)

In the unlikely event that these units were anything like at full strength, this would have given Boniface an army of 11,500 infantry and 9,500 cavalry. This was more or less the same number of troops as the Vandals could have called on, if they had indeed crossed into Africa with 80,000 people. The actual number of soldiers that could be fielded by the Count of Africa was probably much less. Some of the units listed above are also doubly accounted for in the *Notitia*, serving under other commands. For example, the *Equites Scutarii Seniores* is also listed as serving under the Count of Tingitania. Furthermore, none of the units would have been at full strength. Even at the best of times, sickness, death, desertion and recruitment difficulties would deplete the ranks, and these were not the best of times. Probably a number closer to 15,000 or less is a more likely estimate for the number of good Roman troops Boniface could hope to field.

The writings of St Augustine and Olympiodorus indicate that Boniface relied heavily on Gothic troops to fill out the ranks of his army. With the Goths now tucked away in western France, it is highly unlikely he could have called on large numbers of them, unless they had been picked up earlier in Italy. At this time most Roman warlords surrounded themselves with a personal bodyguard of barbarian warriors who swore loyalty to the commander himself. Known as *bucellarii*, these personal troops could be fairly large contingents – almost private armies. In the next century Belisarius, for example, had several thousand such *bucellarii*. We have no idea of the number of personal troops Boniface had been able to surround himself with, but it is likely to have been in the hundreds rather than thousands. Back in 427-8, when Boniface was out of favour at court, one of the delegations sent by Ravenna to bring him to heel was led by Sigisvult, who was backed up by a number of Gothic troops. Possibly some of Sigisvult's men remained behind after their leader went back to Italy just to keep an eye on things. If so, their loyalty to Boniface would have been doubtful and there is some evidence to suggest that they let him down in the battle that followed.

It would be wonderful to have a similar wealth of information to draw on for the Vandal army, but we do not. Numbers and composition can only be guessed at. With nothing better to go on than the original 80,000 people, we can only assume that Geiseric was able to command 15-20,000 warriors. There would certainly have been many casualties in the year that had passed since the Vandals crossed into Africa, and some of his troops may have been dispersed to garrison captured towns. It is also possible that he had been able to gather new recruits along the way. Some of these could have been disaffected Romans and deserters from the Roman Army, and it is also possible that bands of Moors, ancestors of today's Berbers, joined up along the way.

Procopius says: 'The names of the Alans and all the other barbarians, except the Moors, were united in the name of the Vandals. At that time, after the death of Valentinian, Geiseric gained the support of the Moors.'

Valentinian died in 455, so we cannot assume that Geiseric was already able to field Moorish auxiliaries in 430, but it is more than likely that at least some bands of them had thrown in their lot with the Vandals, just as others would have opposed them. No doubt the support of these light skirmishers would have been welcomed, even if not relied on.

So what of the Vandal warriors themselves? How would they have been equipped and how would they have fought? Unfortunately, the migrating Vandals have left no record to help us. Unlike the Franks and Alamanni who remained on the Rhine, there are no warrior graves stocked with weapons and equipment to help us draw any firm conclusions so, once again, any reconstruction of Geiseric's army has to be conjectural.

A 16-year-old, taking up arms for the first time to fight the Franks and then cross the Rhine in 406, would now be 40. If he had survived the long, arduous trek through Gaul, Spain and Africa, he would have fought against Constantine's Romans, Wallia's Goths, Heremigarius' Suevi and no doubt had an encounter or two with the Moors along the way. There would have been very few like him left. Geiseric was a child when he came across the Rhine and most of his *chillarchs* had no memory of life in Germania. However the original Vandals and Alans may have fought before they came into the Roman Empire, their tactics and fighting style would have adapted to huge changes in circumstances since then.

With such short periods of settled peace, most of their equipment would have been begged, borrowed or stolen along the way, with Roman armourers providing as much or more of it than Vandal smiths. There does not seem to have been any sort of division of troops according to fighting style or social class. A warrior was a warrior and as such he fought hand-to-hand, either on foot or horseback depending on the circumstances. We have already seen how a steady supply of trained horses able to stand up to the rigors of battle would have been quite problematic for the Vandals. Even if we accept that they had now been able to round up a good number of horses from the African countryside, the quality would have been quite variable and there would have been no time to train horse and rider together. As the Vandals ranged over the African provinces, the majority would have remained mounted. To assault a town, they would have done so on foot. What they would have done up against Boniface's army, with almost half of the Romans mounted on good, well-trained horses, can only be guessed at. I am inclined to think that many, especially those with inferior mounts, would still have thought it prudent to dismount, form a shieldwall and fight on foot when facing the numerous, well-mounted Roman cavalry.

The most experienced and well equipped men probably formed the front ranks, with lesser warriors falling in behind. Unlike many other Germanic peoples, where the poorer classes were often bow-armed, the

Vandals seem never to have taken to using missile weapons. According to Procopius, this caused them some difficulties in later engagements with the Moors (see Chapter 6) where he says that the Vandals 'were neither good with the javelin nor with the bow.' This is somewhat surprising considering that the original Alans employed a combination of mounted archers and lancers. It may be that as they moved west the lancers came into increasing prominence and the use of horse archery gradually died out. The Alans that Ammianus knew in the fourth century were 'light and active in the use of arms... somewhat like the Huns.' Yet later references emphasise their heavy equipment. For example, Jordanes, in his description of the Battle of Neado in 454, speaks of: 'Goths fighting with lances, the Gepids raging with the sword, the Rugi breaking off the spears in their own wounds, the Suebi fighting on foot, the Huns with bows, the Alans drawing up a battle-line of heavy-armed and the Heruls of light-armed warriors.'

Horse archery is not an easy skill to master. It takes years of practice to develop and maintain. In the changing circumstances of the long migration, it is most likely that the sons of those men who had been proficient horse archers back on the Danube did not have the time nor inclination to pick up the skill. Increasingly, the Alans in the Vandal coalition became exclusively hand-to-hand fighters, just like the Vandals they merged with. It is more than likely that any previous differences between the fighting styles of their Vandal or Alan ancestors had entirely disappeared by the time they crossed into Africa.

In May 430, the two armies met in battle somewhere near Hippo Regius. Probably the Vandals had the largest force, but the numbers must have been fairly close as otherwise Boniface would not have risked battle. We have no details about what occurred other than the fact that the Vandals won, driving Boniface back into the city.

The victorious Vandals invested Hippo Regius in a siege that lasted fourteen months from May 430 until July 431. Leaving us to wonder at the ease in which the Vandals had taken other towns, Hippo Regius held out, although its most famous citizen, St Augustine, died on 28 August 430 with the Vandals at the walls. The biggest dangers in protracted siege operations come from famine and disease. These are equal threats to both the attackers and defenders. Supplied by sea and with plenty of warning to bring in supplies from the hinterland, the defenders of

Hippo Regius seem to have been less affected than the Vandals. By now the surrounding countryside would have been stripped bare of food, so Geiseric would have been forced to leave only minimal troops maintaining the siege lines while the rest of his army and huge train of non-combatants spread out across the province in a neverending search for provisions.

So it was, as Procopius reports:

'After much time had passed by, since they [the Vandals] were unable to secure Hippo Regius either by force or surrender, and since at the same time they were being pressed by hunger, they raised the siege.'

The situation in Africa was now on a knife edge. The Vandals could not afford to lose because one way or another they had come to the end of their journey. There was simply nowhere else to go. The Romans also could not afford to lose as the province was critical to supplying the West with the food and taxes they needed to keep the Empire afloat.

The situation in Africa is neatly summed up by Bishop Capreolus of Carthage explaining to the Synod of Ephesus in July 431 why the African bishops were unable to attend:

'The prompt ability of any that could travel is impeded by the excessive multitude of enemies and the huge devastation of the provinces everywhere which presents to eye-witnesses one place where all its inhabitants have been killed, another where they have been driven into flight, and a wretched vista of destruction spreading out far and wide and in every direction.'

So the Romans made another concerted effort to wrest control of Africa back from the Vandals. Ravenna sent reinforcements from Italy to make good Boniface's losses and Constantinople sent an expeditionary force led by Flavius Ardabur Aspar, who was interestingly both an Arian and of Alan descent. Procopius tells us what happened:

'A little later [in 432] Boniface and the Romans in Libya; since a numerous army had come from both Rome and Byzantium [Constantinople] and Aspar with them as general; decided to renew the struggle. And a fierce battle was fought in which they were badly beaten by the enemy and they made haste to flee as each one could.'

Unfortunately we have no more detail of what happened in this battle, which may have been fought near Carthage, other than what is in Procopius' brief passage. Aspar later became the Eastern Empire's most powerful warlord and was already an experienced military commander. Boniface, despite his defeat at Hippo Regius, also had a very high reputation as a general. So the Roman defeat could not have been down to poor military leadership. Neither could the Romans have been hugely outnumbered, as otherwise they would have avoided battle and waited until the Vandals had been decimated by hunger. The quality of the troops they led must also have been reasonably good, especially those sent from the East which, no doubt, would have been a picked force. Therefore, the Vandal victory must have been down to a combination of Geiseric's leadership and the quality of the men he led, who had been sharpened and hardened over years of arduous campaigning. Clearly the Vandals had come a long way from their early days, when victory in open battle seemed to have eluded them.

This was the victory the Vandals needed and although they did not yet have peace, they were well on the way to achieving their goal of establishing a new homeland. They took Hippo Regius, the citizens no doubt now feeling further resistance was futile. Geiseric made it his capital. Then once again Roman politics intervened to help them further. Boniface was recalled to Italy by Galla Placidia in order to combat Aeitus' growing power. Aeitus was now the West's pre-eminent warlord and an eventual clash between him and Boniface had been brewing for some time. Now, when the Western Romans should have been combining forces to keep Africa, they once again fell to fighting amongst themselves. Boniface defeated Aeitus near Rimini, but was wounded in the battle and later died of his wounds.

Aspar seems to have remained at Carthage for a few more years as, although an Eastern general, he was appointed as the Western Empire's Consul of Africa in 434. He no longer had sufficient strength to take on the Vandals in the field and the Vandals could not take Carthage while it was well garrisoned. Between 432 and 435 there seems to have been a desultory conflict between Geiseric and Aspar, the former now having a secure capital at Hippo Regius with access to the sea and the latter safe behind Carthage's fortifications.

By 435 both sides needed a break. Geiseric wanted what his people had been seeking for years, a formal treaty which gave them a place within the Empire which the Roman authorities recognized. Felix and Boniface were both dead and Aetius was now back in Gaul, campaigning to secure his Gallic power base against the Visigoths, Burgundians and *Baccaudae*. Meanwhile, the Eastern Empire was having serious trouble with the Huns along the Danube frontier and was in no position to continue propping up the West's hold over Africa. So it was in February 435 (although some sources say 436) that a treaty was concluded.

Procopius tells us that the treaty was very much down to Geiseric's initiative:

'After defeating Boniface and Aspar in battle, Geiseric displayed a foresight worth recounting, whereby he made his good fortune thoroughly secure. For fearing lest, if once again an army should come against him from both Rome and Byzantium, the Vandals might not be able to use the same strength and enjoy the same fortune.... He was not lifted up by the good fortune he had enjoyed, but rather became moderate because of what he feared and so he made a treaty with the Emperor Valentinian providing that each year he should pay the Emperor tribute from Libya and he delivered one of his sons, Huneric, as a hostage to make this agreement binding. So Geiseric both showed himself a brave man in battle and guarded the victory as securely as possible.'

This probably mixes up the terms of this treaty with a later one in 442, since Huneric went to Ravenna as a hostage at the later date. Be that as it may, the terms of this treaty recognised the status quo, giving the Vandals official status as *foederati* within the lands they had taken by force in return for tribute and leaving Carthage free from attack. Technically, *foederati,* or federate status, meant land in exchange for military service, but neither side would have been under any illusion that this was the case here. As with the Goths in Aquitaine, the Vandals now

1. The Hornhausen relief is a rare depiction of a mounted Germanic warrior who would have been typical of most later Vandal warriors. Many or most early Vandals probably fought on foot. *(Landesmuseum für Vorgeschichte, Halle)*

2. Silver spurs from a third-century Germanic noble's grave in Leuna, Germany. They were possibly made from recycled Roman silver. Many of the early Vandals probably fought on foot but as the lesser warriors were cremated, we do not have detailed knowledge of their equipment. *(British Museum, author's photo)*

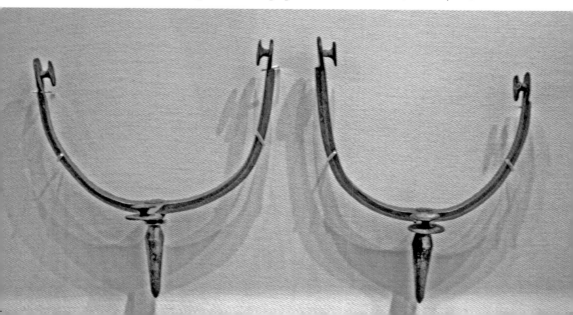

3. These Sarmatian warriors depicted on Trajan's column were the ancestors of the Alans who joined up with the Vandals. They were noted as heavily armoured cavalrymen and although some early Alans may also have been mounted archers, horse archery died out amongst those Alans who migrated with the Vandals into Spain and Africa. *(Trajan's Column, Rome, author's photo).*

4. This magnificent gilded Roman cavalry helmet from Deurne in the Netherlands is of a style that may also have been worn by wealthier Vandal warriors. Most Vandal arms and equipment came from Roman sources after they crossed the Rhine. A prestige piece of equipment such as this would have been a warrior's prized possession.

(Rijksmuseum voor Oudheden, Leiden, photo Michiel)

5. This page from a medieval copy of the *Notitia Dignitatum* shows the cities under the control of the *Dux Mogontiacensis*. With his headquarters at Mogontiacum (Mainz), he was the Roman officer responsible for the defence of the middle Rhine frontier where the Vandals crossed on the last day of 406. *(Notitia Dignitatum, Bodleian manuscript)*

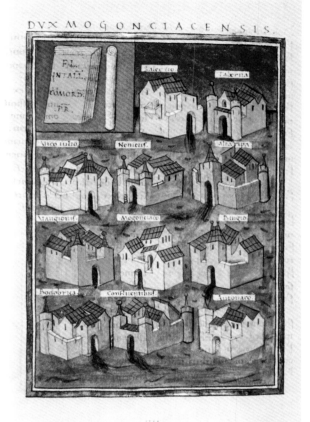

6. A reconstructed ship of the Roman Rhine fleet. Such ships helped to protect the frontier. *(The Museum of Ancient Shipping, Mainz)*

7. This carving from around 395 depicts the half-Vandal general Stilicho, his wife, Serena, and son, Eucherius. Stilicho was widely criticised after his death for having let the Vandals into the Empire and then not taking any steps to defeat them. There is, however, no evidence of collusion. *(Monza Cathedral)*

8. This stele is thought to show an Alan. Wearing scale armour and carrying a lance, he would have been a formidable opponent in hand-to-hand combat. Although many Vandals probably had shields and shorter lances they did not use missile weapons. They often found themselves at a loss when confronted by the more lightly equipped Moors. *(Hermitage Museum, St Petersburg)*

9. In 425 the Vandals raided the Balearic Isles and North African coast, probably commandeering fishing boats such as the one depicted here on a North African mosaic. *(Bardo Museum, author's photo)*

10. Transporting cavalry horses by sea was not impossible as this North African mosaic depicts. However, it would have required specialist transport ships, which the Vandals are unlikely to have possessed in 429. Most likely only a few horses came with them across the Straights of Gibraltar. *(Bardo Museum, author's photo)*

11. The province of Africa Proconsularis was the most prosperous region of the West Roman Empire in the early fifth century. Luxurious villas, such as this of the Dominus Julius outside Carthage, provided food and taxes to keep the Empire running. *(Bardo Museum, author's photo)*

12. Luxury ceramics known as
African *sigillata*, characterised
by its red slip, were exported all
over the Roman Empire.
(Bardo Museum, author's photo)

14. This fifth-century wood carving from
Egypt shows Roman soldiers defending a city
from marauding tribesmen. With a garrison
such as this, the city of Hippo Regius was
able to hold out against the Vandals in 430-31.
(Museum für Byzantinische Kunst, Berlin)

13. North Africa provided much of the produce that kept the West Roman
Empire alive. This mosaic from Hadrumentum (Sousse) shows a merchant ship
being offloaded and food supplies being weighed. *(Bardo Museum, author's photo)*

PRO CONSVL AFRICAE

Sub dispositione uiri spectabilis proconsulis Africe

Ramea æ-cosularis   agentii iiiib;   Comentariesез   Exceptores
æ-legatieuifduo.   duodenarium   Adiutore   Singulares
Officiiante   Cornicilarium   Abacus   æ-reliquum
habet ita   Numerariofduo.   Subadiuuas.   officium,-
Primape de scola   frumsciium

15. This frontispiece from the *Notitia Dignitatum* emphasises the prosperity of Africa Proconsularis and the importance of maritime trade. The Comes Africae was the Roman official responsible for the defence of the Region with an army of 11,500 infantry and 9,500 cavalry at full strength. Boniface, who held the office in 429, was defeated by the Vandals in battle.
(Notitia Dignitatum, Bodleian manuscript)

16. A silver plate celebrating the appointment of Flavius Ardabur Aspar as Consul of Africa in 434. Aspar was defeated in battle by Geiseric but briefly held onto Carthage under the terms of the treaty of 435.
(National Archaeological Museum, Florence, photo by Sailko)

17. The ruins of Roman Carthage. The Vandals failed to take the city as long as it was well garrisoned but seized it in a surprise attack in 439. It then became their capital. *(Antonine Baths, Carthage, author's photo)*

18. A necklace and earrings from the so-called Carthage Treasure, which was buried by the Cresconii family for safekeeping, probably when Geiseric attacked the city in 429. This combination of emeralds, sapphires and pearls was held in such high esteem that the Emperor Leo (447-474) restricted the wearing of such jewels to the Imperial family in later years. *(British Museum, author's photo)*

19. A fifth-century funerary mosaic
depicting a Roman banker from
Thabraca (Tabarka) in Numidia.
After the Vandal conquest Roman
officials continued to administer the
bureaucracy, gather taxes and keep
things running in a profitable manner.
(Bardo Museum, author's photo)

20. This fifth-century funeral mosaic
also from Thrabraca is of a ship owner
by the name of Felix. Men such as he
would have provided the expertise
which enabled the Vandals to build a
powerful fleet.
(Bardo Museum, author's photo)

21. The gravestone of a priest from the Basilica of Vitalis (Sbeitla) in Byzacena. He died on 12 September 467 in the twenty-eighth year of Geiseric's reign. The Vandals vigourously persecuted the Roman orthodox clergy.
(Bardo Museum, author's photo)

22. This fourth-century mosaic from Dougga in North Africa depicts Ulysses tied to a mast to resist the Sirens. The single-banked galley carrying men equipped as late Roman soldiers would have been the sort of ships that took part in the failed expedition to reconquer Africa from the Vandals in 468.
(Bardo Museum, author's photo)

23. This surviving fragment of the column of Arcadius in Constantinople is a rare depiction of a fifth-century East Roman infantryman. Men such as this would have taken part in the 468 expedition.
(Istanbul Archeological Museum, author's photo)

24. The military port of Carthage could accommodate 220 warships in its heyday. Civilian ships were harboured in an adjoining port. Geiseric probably had around 300 ships under his command when he took control of the Western Mediterranean. *(Port of Carthage, author's photo)*

25. This painting by Karl Briullov (1799–1852) depicts the Vandals' fourteen-day sack of Rome in 455. It captures the popular image of modern times with savage barbarians and dark skinned 'Moors' carrying off helpless maidens, including the widow and daughters of the late Emperor. Few of the details are correct, however the figure of Pope Leo in negotiation with Geiseric is not far from the truth. The terms of the sack were worked out between the two outside the walls. Although the Vandals carried off everything of value, including the Imperial women and many other captives, there was probably less bloodshed than there would have been otherwise. *(Tretyakov Gallery, Moscow)*

26. This fragment of a large mosaic pavement from Carthage, shows a Vandal horseman riding in front of a villa he has appropriated from its former Roman owner. His clothing, including bare upper legs, shows how the Vandals adopted Roman styles suitable for the North African climate but his long hair marks him out as a Vandal. The brand on the horse's rear, known as the tamga, is thought to be typical of the Sarmatians. As the Alans were a Sarmatian people this may have been an Alan tradition. Other mosaics depict horses with the same brand. *(British Museum, author's photo)*

27. Another mosaic fragment from Carthage depicting a Vandal hunting. Procopius says that the Vandals clothed themselves in silk garments, 'and passed their time, thus dressed, in hippodromes and in other pleasurable pursuits, and above all else in hunting'. *(British Museum)*

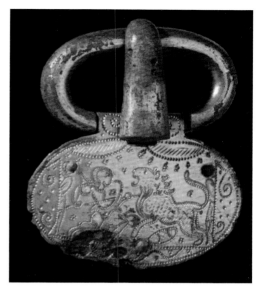

29. The engraving on this sixth-century Vandal belt buckle depicts a lion hunt, shows how the Vandals had adopted the lifestyles of the Roman aristocracy once they had settled in Africa.
(British Museum, author's photo)

28. These items from a Vandal woman's grave in North Africa show a mix of influences. The amber beads may be heirlooms from her original central European homeland. The gold and garnet earrings are of typical Germanic style, while the disk broaches show Mediterranean influences.
(British Museum, author's photo)

30. The Moors were lightly equipped, fast moving cavalry and infantry who caused the Vandals no end of trouble after Geiseric's death. Although this detail is from Trajan's coloumn, they probably did not change much in appearance over the centuries.
(Trajan's column Rome, author's photo)

31. A Vandal coin, probably from Gelimer's reign, depicting a Vandal warrior which may be a likeness of the king himself. It shows many classical influences, including the horse head which was a common symbol of the ancient Carthaginians. *(British Museum)*

32. A reconstruction of a *dromon*, one of the small, fast galleys that protected Belisarius' armada on the long voyage from Constantinople to Africa. It is likely that the Vandals also had such ships in their navy, although the majority were probably simple troop transports. Larger galleys were no longer in use at the time of the Vandals. *(Model Ship Master)*

33. This mosaic from Ravenna depicts the Emperor Justinian surrounded by ecclesiastic and secular officials as well as Roman guardsmen. Created in the mid-540's after the reconquest of Africa and Italy, it is an evocative statement of Justinian's power. The bearded man standing at Justinian's right-hand side (on the left from the viewer's perspective) could be Belisarius. *(Church of San Vitale, Ravenna)*

34. A silver dish from Isola Rizza near Verona probably depicting a sixth-century East Roman soldier riding down a Lombard. The Roman's weapons and equipment show Alan influences and many men in both Gelimer's and Belisarius' armies would have looked quite similar. Most Vandals probably carried a shield and spear rather than the two-handed lance. *(photo James Steakley)*

35. This sixth-century Egyptian ivory shows late Roman troops. In the middle is a horse archer armed and equipped as described by Procopius. The Vandals had no tactical response to such troops who could both skirmish and fight in hand-to-hand combat. *(Rheinisches Landes Museum Trier)*

36. This hunting scene from the late fifth/early sixth-century probably depicts a Vandal. Although seemingly Roman in appearance, the way he wears his cloak and the undecorated tunic are different from Roman fashions. The loose, long trousers seem to have been quite common amongst Germanic warriors at the time of Justinian's re-conquests. It is most unlikely than any Romans in North Africa would have remained in possession of their old grand estates. *(Bardo Museum, author's photo)*

37. When Gelimer marched on Carthage prior to the Battle of Tricamarum in December 533, he cut the aqueduct that supplied the city with water. Water supplies held out as Carthage had twenty-four huge water cisterns capable of storing over 50 million litres of water. *(La Malga, Tunisia, author's photo)*

had a de facto independent kingdom, with Hippo Regius as its capital and most of Numidia and a western sliver of Africa Proconsularis under their jurisdiction. Aspar was then recalled to Constantinople, Aetius was able to focus all his attention on Gaul and the Vandals could recoup their strength, laying the foundations of their new kingdom.

Chapter 5

Mare Nostrum

Carthago Delenda Est

The treaty of 435 seemed to give Geiseric what he wanted and maybe when he signed on the dotted line he felt happy with the settlement, or perhaps he just wanted to recoup his strength before going further. The Romans probably thought that they were merely buying a breathing space and as long as they still controlled Carthage and the surrounding countryside, there was still some revenue coming from Africa. They also had a bridgehead to use once other pressing matters had been dealt with, such as the barbarians and *Baccaudae* in Gaul and the Huns on the Danube. Africa was simply too valuable to be given up easily, but with Aeitus firmly focused on Gaul, it was Constantinople rather than Ravenna where plans to retake Africa were being formulated.

So the treaty of 435 to carve up Africa was probably not dissimilar to Hitler and Stalin's agreement to partition Poland in 1940. Neither side trusted the other, the peace could not possibly last but it gave Geiseric time to build his strength and allowed the Romans (both East and West) to take care of other matters.

Beyond giving them the opportunity to persecute Catholic bishops and appropriate their wealth, this phoney peace also gave the Vandals the time and means to build a fleet. Their experiences in the latter years of their time in Spain and the crossing into Africa had shown them the value of sea power. Transporting supplies over land in ox-drawn wagons was slow, cumbersome and expensive, whereas by sea it could be done far more easily. From Hippo Regius, Roman merchantmen had regularly sailed with food and goods to supply Italy and Gaul. Now many of the ships, their builders and sailors were in Vandal hands. Quite probably, Geiseric had used some of the ships he had appropriated in Spain to support him on the long march to Hippo Regius, but now he had both the time and local expertise to expand on this.

Geiseric also needed to keep his followers constantly rewarded with wealth and prestige to maintain their loyalty. No doubt some were happy to settle down as gentlemen farmers lording it over the local population, but many, especially the younger ones who had known nothing but constant warfare all their lives, would have been looking for opportunities to carve a name for themselves with force of arms. Whatever Geiseric's long-term plan had been when he signed the peace treaty in 435, it was the Vandals who broke it, using their new-found sea power to raid Sicily in 438.

One of the Roman stereotypes of barbarians was that they would not keep treaties, and the Vandals seemed to live up to this. Bishop Quodvultdeus of Carthage had this to say of them in the 430s: 'While you void or cast off the struggles to lend assistance, you are neither brave in war, nor are you faithful in peace.'

The bishop's words proved prophetic. Without warning, Geiseric suddenly struck east and took Carthage on 19 October 439. The ease at with which he did this is astounding. Hippo Regius had held out for fourteen months in 430/431, and after defeating Boniface and Aspar the Vandals were never able to breach Carthage's walls. In both cases, however, the Romans had good troops within the walls and were fully expecting an attack. Perhaps they had been lulled into complacency after the treaty, but even if the bulk of Boniface and Aspar's troops had been withdrawn in 432 and 435 respectively, it is inconceivable that the Romans would have left Carthage without an adequate garrison.

Quodvultdeus gives us plenty of gruesome details of what happened once the Vandals were inside the walls: 'Horrible death has soiled all the streets... pregnant women slaughtered... babies taken from the arms of their nurse and thrown to die on the street...the cries of those that have lost in this assault a husband or a father.' Unfortunately, neither he nor any other tell us how it happened, although Quodvultdeus' lament does imply that there was an assault.

It could really only have been a surprise attack, prepared and executed without the Romans hearing of it and the Vandals inside the walls before the garrison knew what was happening. If the gates were barred, then the city would have been able to hold out for quite some time, even if the garrison was relatively small. This does not appear to have been the case. If a traitor or dissident Arian had opened the gates, or if a deal had been struck as was the case at Rome in 455, then surely the chroniclers would have had something to say about it. But they don't.

However Carthage fell, the result was that it left the Vandals as the undisputed masters of Roman Africa – previously the most prosperous region of the West Roman Empire. In a reverse parallel to the fate of many poor migrants from Africa today, Quodvultdeus and other Catholic clergy were packed onto rickety boats and sent to Italy with the expectation that they would sink enroute, although in the end they made it. The Vandals availed themselves of the riches of the nobles and the Catholic Church, suddenly finding themselves elevated from a desperate band of migrants to one of the most powerful kingdoms in the Mediterranean world.

Pirates of the Mediterranean

The brief interlude at Hippo Regius had given the Vandals their first real opportunity to begin to build a fleet. The capture of Carthage, the second most important port in the Western Mediterranean after Rome's Portus, catapulted them into becoming a first-rate sea power. With the great port – originally built by the Carthaginians and improved by the Romans – along with some of the best shipbuilders and sailors in the world now in their hands, the Vandals had all the capability they needed, even though they 'were previously unaccustomed with the use of ships' to re-use Prosper's words.

There was now no pretence of federate status. The Vandals were a new and independent nation free to rule North Africa as they wished, impose their Arian version of Christianity and expand their power and wealth at Rome's expense. From 440 onwards, they raided the coasts of Sicily. They captured Marsala, laid siege to Palermo and even plundered Bruttium in southern Italy. Now that they had a homeland to call their own, these raids were no longer an attempt to take new territory but rather to amass greater wealth and to give the young warriors a chance to make a name for themselves. According to Hydatius, Geiseric was also encouraged into Sicily by the Arian Maximinus, who incited the Vandals to persecute Catholics there.

Procopius evocatively described the state of Vandal piracy that lasted for more than thirty years:

'Every year, at the beginning of spring Geiseric made invasions into Sicily and Italy, enslaving some of the cities, razing others to the ground, and plundering everything. When the land had become destitute of men and of money, he invaded the domain of the Emperor of the East. And so he plundered Illyricum (modern Croatia), most of the Peloponnese and the rest of Greece, and all of the Islands which lie near it. And then he went off again to Sicily and Italy and kept plundering and pillaging all places in turn. One day when he had embarked on his ship in the harbour of Carthage, and the sails were ready to be spread, the pilot asked him against what men did he go? And in reply he said: "Plainly against those with whom God is angry."'

In Italy the Imperial authorities were forced to implement special measures. Various edicts in Valentinian's name show that taxes were increased, local peasants given permission to bear arms, city walls were improved and the Master of Soldiers, Sigisvult (the same man who had been sent to deal with Boniface in 427), was tasked with bolstering coastal defences.

Rome could not allow this situation to continue unchecked, but while Africa should have been the focus of the Western Empire it no longer had the strength or will to do anything other than try to defend the coast of Italy. Aetius was the last remaining West Roman warlord. He seems to have turned his back on Italy and Africa, employing an army of Huns to maintain control over Gaul. Therefore it fell to the East Romans to take action.

In 440, Constantinople prepared a huge invasion fleet with the intention of retaking Africa, ending the piracy and restoring the 'universal church'. There are some indications that this may have been a joint operation between the two halves of the Empire with the rendezvous being Sicily, which the Romans from both halves of the Empire, would use as a staging point before moving onto Carthage. An edict issued in the name of Valentinian III from June 440 hints at this: 'The army of the most invincible Emperor Theodosius our Father [the Eastern Emperor], will soon approach and…. We trust that the Most Excellent Patrician

Aetius will soon be here with a large force.' This may, however, have been wishful thinking on the part of Valentinian's courtiers rather than a statement of fact.

In 441, a large fleet set sail from Constantinople for Sicily. It is said to have contained 1,100 ships, but as this is exactly the same number of ships given for the better documented 468 expedition, it seems slightly suspicious. However many ships there were, there were certainly a lot of them and we can probably expect that an invasion would not have been contemplated with much less than 15–20,000 soldiers. Fortunately for the Vandals, this army was led by five generals who apparently did not get along. Even more fortunately, Rome's old opponents were stirring beyond the eastern frontiers.

As soon as the fleet set sail, the Eastern Empire's enemies decided to take advantage of this sudden exodus of troops. The Persians invaded Roman Armenia and the Huns poured over the Danube frontier, devastating the Balkans and even threatening Constantinople. Having reached Sicily, but apparently accomplishing very little, the expeditionary force was recalled to deal with these new, more pressing dangers.

Abandoned by the East, with cash running out and Aetius busy in Gaul, the Emperor Valentinian III had no choice but to agree to another treaty which recognized the new Vandal conquests. The Western Empire formally ceded control of Carthage and all of Africa Proconsularis in exchange for the Vandals agreeing to continue the grain supply to Italy, no doubt at a handsome profit to themselves. The enlarged Vandal kingdom also included Byzacena, the province to the south of Carthage, and parts of western Tripolitania to the east. Apparently the long strip of the Mauretanias, through which the Vandals had marched in 429/30, was left under Roman control.

Geiseric was now elevated to the status of client king with the title *Rex Socius et Amicus*. It was probably at this time too that his son, Huneric, went as a hostage to Ravenna and there he was betrothed to Valentinian's infant daughter, Eudocia. There was just one tiny problem, however, which was that Huneric was already married to the daughter of Theodoric, King of the Goths of Aquitaine. Not letting a previous royal alliance interfere with a better match, Geiseric had the unfortunate woman returned to her father. Relations between the Vandals and Goths, whom we should probably now call 'Visigoths' to distinguish them from their 'Ostrogoth' cousins who are about to show up on the scene, had never been good. This started a feud which would last decades. According to Jordanes, it was one of the underlying reasons the Visigoths stood alongside the Romans when Attila invaded Gaul in 451:

'When Geiseric, King of the Vandals, learned that Attila's mind was bent on the devastation of the world, he incited him by many gifts to make war on the Visigoths, for he was afraid that Theodoric, king of the Visigoths, would avenge the injury done to his daughter. She had been joined in wedlock with Huneric, Geiseric's son, and at first was happy in this union. But afterwards he was cruel even to his own children, and because of the mere suspicion that she was attempting to poison him, he cut off her nose and mutilated her ears. He sent her back to her father in Gaul thus despoiled of her natural charms. So the wretched girl presented a pitiable aspect ever after, and the cruelty which would stir even strangers still more surely incited her father to vengeance.'

Whether or not this is true we cannot know. It is unlikely that a ruler as canny as Geiseric would have gone out of his way to provoke Theodoric unnecessarily. However, Geiseric did face a revolt amongst his nobles in 442, probably brought about by the amount of power and wealth he had been reserving for himself. In the Germanic tradition the king was a war leader and gift giver. As his wealth and personal prestige increased, Geiseric was taking on the trappings of Imperial power along with the lofty titles granted him by the Emperor. We do not have much detail of this revolt, but Prosper of Aquitaine tells us that it resulted in more dead Vandals than defeat in war. Possibly the unfortunate Visigoth princess became mixed up in this and paid a horrible price.

The treaty of 442 did not put an end to Vandal piracy, but it would appear that Geiseric was careful not to push the boundaries of his agreement with Valentinian III. Perhaps the West Romans tacitly gave the Vandals a free hand at sea so long as the grain shipments continued to reach Italy. Procopius tells us that relations between Carthage and Ravenna improved greatly while Hydatius reports that, in 445, a Vandal fleet raided Turonium on the Atlantic coast of Suevian-held Gallaecia. If the latter report is correct, then it was a most daring undertaking which involved sailing thousands of miles from modern Tunisia, through the Straits of Gibraltar and up the coast of modern Portugal. Such an expedition could not have been undertaken with rickety old commandeered boats, but rather with good ocean-going ships. Possibly Geiseric wanted to give his more adventurous young men an outlet for their warlike spirits without prejudicing his treaty with Valentinian. A kick at his old enemies in Gallaecia probably took care of both.

We should not, however, think of the Vandal fleet as an armada of warships in the mould of the great navies of classical Greece, Rome and Carthage. The Mediterranean had been a Roman lake for centuries and the need for powerful *quinqueremes* to engage enemy battle ships had long disappeared. For the most part the Vandal fleet would have been made up of troop-carrying transports which ferried warriors and supplies to their destination and dropped them off, much like the Viking raiders of later times. In 533, a Vandal fleet of 120 ships carried 5000 warriors to Sardinia, so each transport was probably capable of carrying on average fifty men, with some of that space taken up for supplies and equipment. Sometimes horses may also have been taken, but it is reasonable to assume that in most cases the Vandals would have not done so unless they intended more than a simple coastal raid, such as the attack on Rome in 455. When Belisarius sailed from Constantinople to Africa, his fleet was protected by a number of fast, light galleys called *dromons*. The Vandals probably also used such vessels, crewed by Romans with a small number of Vandal 'marines' onboard.

With neither the Romans nor Vandals possessing many true warships and the art of war at sea largely forgotten, there were virtually no sea battles. Actions at sea probably resembled the sort of pirate actions which go on off the coast of Somalia today rather than great naval engagements. There is one battle we do have details of – that is the defeat of the East Roman fleet by the Vandals in 468. Much like the English victory over the Spanish Armada in 1588, this was done by attacking the Roman fleet at anchor with fire ships. There was also a sea battle off Corsica in 456 in which the Romans were victorious, but unfortunately we do not have any information about what happened there.

No doubt the Vandal ships were built and crewed by Roman North Africans. It is impossible to say how many sailors this involved. A Roman *dromon* probably had 120 rowers. Many of the Vandal ships were more likely to have been transports, some of which operated under sail alone, therefore requiring a much smaller crew. For the most part, the Vandals' piratical exploits in the Mediterranean probably involved less than 100 ships carrying a couple of thousand warriors at most, with larger expeditions being the exception. Probably the largest fleet gathered was for Geiseric's attack on Rome in 455, when he had to have enough vessels to carry the best part of his army, along with horses and supplies, and then bring the captives and loot back home again. This probably required something close to 300 ships. In a sideways tribute to Vandal seamanship, Procopius says that only one ship was lost and this was on the way home as a result of it being overloaded with large statues and stolen loot.

So why didn't the West Romans go to the archives, dust off the plans from Octavian's and Mark Antony's fleets at Actium half a millennia ago, then build themselves a navy to take on the Vandals?

They simple answer is that they could not afford to.

Modern estimates equate the annual financial loss to the treasury from the Vandal takeover of North Africa to be the same amount it would have cost to keep 40,000 soldiers in the field for a year. If we add in the losses from Britain, Spain and Gaul, then it is easy to see how the Empire could no longer maintain its standing army, let alone start to build a war fleet from scratch. It also helps to explain why barbarian federates became an increasingly attractive option. If you could not afford to pay soldiers, why not give them some land and let them maintain themselves on it in lieu of pay?

Constantinople did still have the resources to build a large fleet and they did do just that on several occasions. The first few attempts ended in disaster, creating both financial and military problems for the Eastern Empire as a consequence.

Geiseric's Kingdom

Geiseric used the peace that followed the treaty of 442 to consolidate his power, keep his nobles in check and set up a system of government that allowed him to rule over a subject population that probably outnumbered the Vandals 40:1. Unlike the American-led coalition in Iraq in 2003, Geiseric did not dismantle the Roman apparatus of government. Roman officials continued to administer the bureaucracy and without their help he could not possibly have managed his far-flung domains, gather taxes and keep things running in a profitable manner. Many Romans held key positions in his government, the main requirement being loyalty to their new masters, which had to be demonstrated by adherence to the Arian version of Christianity. They were, however, excluded from the army, although Romans probably crewed the fleet.

Geiseric made no attempt to integrate Romans and Vandals into a single nation. The Vandals were the masters and the Romans were the subjects. They were kept apart not only by religion but also by law. The Vandals adopted Roman-style clothing such as highly decorated, light linen tunics suitable for the African climate. Mosaics from North Africa show Vandals looking very similar to Romans of that time, but they reserved certain aspects of dress and appearance for themselves only. Victor of Vita tells us that the Vandals wore their hair long in contrast to the short hair styles of the Romans. This seems to have been common with other Germanic peoples as several monuments show long-haired German troops alongside short-haired Romans. If a Roman adopted Vandal long hair styles and was seen in a Catholic church, his hair would be pulled out as a punishment.

The estates of the large Roman landowners were confiscated. Catholic churches were closed and their property was also used to fill Geiseric's coffers and reward his followers. It was these actions which resulted in our sources speaking so vehemently about the horrors of the Vandal occupation, as it was the clergy and nobility who suffered greatly. The writers of our original sources came from these groups. Probably, for the vast mass of lower class Roman citizens and slaves, their condition did not change greatly with the new masters at the top. If anything their tax burdens may have decreased and, so long as they were not committed Catholics, the peace of 442 would have been vastly better than the years of violent conflict that had preceded it.

Procopius gives us a detailed account of how Geiseric went about land redistribution:

'Among the Libyans all who happened to be men of note and conspicuous for their wealth he [Geiseric] handed over as slaves, together with their estates and all their money to his sons.... And he robbed the rest of the Libyans of their estates which were both very numerous and excellent, and distributed them among the nation of the Vandals. As a result of this, these lands have been called 'Vandal Estates' up to the present time. And it fell to the lot of those who had formerly possessed these lands to be in extreme poverty and to be at the same time free men.

'Geiseric commanded that all the lands which he had given over to his sons and the other Vandals should not be subject to any kind of taxation. But as much of the lands did not seem as good to him he allowed to remain in the hands of their former owners but assessed so large a sum to be paid on this land in taxes that nothing whatsoever remained to those who retained their farms. And many of them were sent into exile or killed.... Thus the Libyans were visited with every form of misfortune.'

He also says that Geiseric dismantled the walls protecting the African towns and cities:

'Geiseric devised the following scheme: he tore down the walls of all the cities in Libya except Carthage so that neither the Libyans themselves, espousing the cause of the Romans, might have a strong base from which to begin a rebellion, nor those sent by the Emperor have any ground for hoping to capture a city and by establishing a new garrison in it, to make trouble for the Vandals.'

This seems to have been a rather odd thing to do, especially as he was no doubt fully expecting another Roman counterattack before too long. However, Geiseric and his Vandals concentrated their settlement in and around Carthage. There were simply not enough of them to spread themselves thinly throughout all of North Africa. They were not just the new ruling class; they were also the army and Geiseric had to be able to muster them to defend Carthage – the jewel in his crown. It made sense for him to concentrate his men on the most profitable estates of Proconsularis and leave the poorer lands to his Roman subjects, as Procopius describes. Had he left fortified towns in these regions then he could have reasonably expected rebels at some time or another to occupy them and use them as a stronghold against him. As ever, each action has a consequence, as Procopius explains: 'In later times, these cities being without walls, were captured all the more easily by Belisarius and with less exertion.'

Romans were not the only inhabitants of Vandal North Africa. The Moors, the original inhabitants, still roamed the far-flung districts, paying no more heed to the Vandal borders than they had to the previous Roman ones. With the disappearance of the Roman *limitanei* along the frontiers they were more or less able to come and go as they pleased, with some bands raiding the less defended regions and others joining up with the Vandals as auxiliaries. Geiseric's policy of removing city walls made his successors' defence against the Moors that much more difficult.

The Sack of Rome

While Geiseric was consolidating his kingdom, the Western Empire was torn apart by the Huns. In 451, Attila invaded Gaul and was checked at the Battle of the Catalaunian Fields by Aeitus and Theodoric's Visigoths, near Troyes in modern France. The Vandals were not involved, but if we are to believe Jordanes there was some sort of agreement between Geiseric and Attila. The following year, Attila invaded Italy, but was forced back through a combination of plague, the intervention of Pope Leo and, more importantly, the arrival of an East Roman Army. In 453, Attila died and his empire fell apart. The following year Aetius was murdered by Valentinian III, and the year after that Valentinian himself was murdered by two of Aetius's former bodyguards. Theodoric the Visigothic King died on the Catalaunian Fields and his son, Thorismund, was busy trying to establish his authority while his two younger brothers hovered around the throne waiting for their chance.

There was now only one strong man and one stable state left within what had been the West Roman Empire. That was Geiseric and the Vandal Kingdom of Africa. Britain had been lost to the Angles and Saxons; much of Spain was in the hands of the Suevi; Gaul was being contested by the Visigoths, Franks, Alamanni, Burgundians and *Baccaudae*; while in Italy, the potential successors to Valentinian's empty throne made their plays for power.

In Rome, Petronius Maximus seized the throne and one of the first things he did was to marry Eudoxia, Valentinian's widow, and marry off Eudocia to his son Palladius. Eudocia was the daughter of Valentinian

III who had been promised to Geiseric's son Huneric. And Geiseric was not best pleased.

Although the Vandals and other barbarians had a reputation amongst the Romans for not keeping treaties, much of this may have stemmed from different views on the nature of such agreements. For the Germans, oaths of loyalty were very personal matters and were sworn between individuals. They had no concept of the enduring state. Geiseric may have pushed the boundaries of his treaty with Valentinian, but he did not blatantly break it. It does appear as though he did break the treaty of 435, but then, although we do not know the details, he may have made it with Aspar. Once Aspar had left, perhaps Geiseric considered the agreement at an end.

Be that as it may, Valentinian was now dead. Petronius had seized power and had taken Huneric's fiancée. This made him Geiseric's personal enemy and, ever ready to seize the opportunity of the moment, the Vandal king moved quickly. He assembled his army and fleet, set sail for Rome and captured Sardinia for good measure along the way. In late May or early June 455, just three months after Valentinian's murder, the Vandal fleet arrived at Portus, the port of Rome. Petronius and many of the Roman nobility panicked and prepared to flee, but the Roman mob took matters into their own hands. Petronius was deserted by his bodyguard and was torn apart by the mob, with bits of him being thrown into the Tiber.

Rome was well protected by walls and its potential to resist a siege is well attested by the long drawn-out affairs of the Gothic wars of the mid-sixth century. Here we now get a glimpse of the sort of thing that may well have happened when the Vandals took so many other walled cities in the past with relative ease. With few, if any, regular soldiers in Rome and no experienced military leader, the terrified citizens feared that resistance was futile. Above all they wanted to avoid the horror of a sack, which would inevitably follow a failed defence of the walls.

Prosper of Aquitaine tells us what happened:

'Holy Pope Leo ran out to meet [Geiseric] outside the gates and, with God's help, by his supplication so softened him that he abstained from fire, slaughter and torture, on the condition that all power was given to him. Therefore, during fourteen days of free and secure searching,

Rome was emptied of her wealth and many thousands of captives. …
Geiseric took Eudoxia captive, together with Eudocia and Placidia the
children of herself and Valentinian, and placing an exceedingly great
treasure in his ships sailed for Carthage, having spared neither bronze
not anything else whatsoever in the palace.'

On their triumphant return to Carthage, the Vandals celebrated the
marriage of Huneric and Eudocia, an event which linked the Asding
line with the Imperial house of Theodosius, of which Valentinian's two
daughters were the last survivors. Although Huneric could never hope
to become Emperor, if he and Eudocia had a male child, he would have
as good a claim as any to the Imperial throne and a better one than
most. Geiseric held onto Valentinian's widow, Eudoxia, and the younger
daughter, Placidia, for seven years. He treated them well but knew their
value as hostages. Eventually he released them to Constantinople. What
he got in exchange we do not know, but the West Romans did appeal to
the Eastern Emperor Marcian for support against the Vandals and none
was forthcoming. Amongst the other notable captives from Rome was
Gaudentius, Aetius's son. Unfortunately, we do not know what became of
him. When Boniface's son, Sebastian, showed up in Vandal territory a few
years earlier, he was executed when he refused to convert to Arianism. No
doubt a similar fate also befell Gaudentius, whether or not a conversion
option was offered.

The West's Last Gasp

The Vandals did not have everything their own way. In the year following
the sack of Rome, Ricimer came to take Aetius' vacant place as the
Western Empire's warlord. He was the grandson of Wallia, the Gothic
king who attacked the Vandals in 416, and his mother was Suevi. So
there was no love lost between his family and the Vandals. He pursued
war against them with new vigour, defeating a fleet of sixty Vandal ships
off Corsica in 456. In the following year, his troops had some success in
a skirmish against Vandal raiders in Campania.

Becoming the new power behind the western throne, Ricimer deposed
the new Emperor Avitus and installed Majorian in his place. Majorian
and Ricimer had plenty of other problems to deal with apart from the

Vandals but the reconquest of Africa was vital for the Western Empire's survival and became the focus of their policies. If they could retake Africa, then food and money would become available once more. If they failed... well, we know what happened in the end.

Majorian made preparations for an invasion, which he intended to launch from Spain, possibly because the more obvious crossing via Sicily had become too hot. After all, if the Vandals had managed it why could the Romans not do the same while they still held on to the western African provinces? The Gallic aristocrat and prolific writer, Sidonius Apollinaris, describes in his flowery anachronistic style how Majorian 'felled the forests of the Apennines and filled the harbours with Roman triremes.' By the spring of 460, the West Romans had gathered a large army and fleet of 300 ships at Cartagena.

Typically, Geiseric did not passively sit by and wait for the invasion to happen. He led his own fleet along the coast of the Mauretanias, poisoning wells and denying provisions along the potential enemy line of march – the same route he had led his people along as a young man. Then somehow – we have no details of what actually happened – he destroyed Majorian's fleet before the West Roman invasion got off the ground. It was a stunning victory and it is a shame that we have no idea how Geiseric was able to pull it off. The result spelt the end for Majorian and any chance of future offensive action by the West Romans. The Western Empire was finished unless the East Romans came to their aid.

In 468 they did just that.

The Battle of Mercurium and the End of Empire

By this time the political landscape had changed considerably. Ricimer executed Majorian but the elderly senator, Libius Severus, whom Ricimer put up in his place, proved unacceptable to Constantinople. In 465, Severus conveniently died and negotiations began between the Eastern Emperor Leo and Ricimer for a mutually acceptable replacement. Geiseric also had a view. When he sent Valentinian's widow and youngest daughter to Constantinople three years earlier, Placidia was married off to the senator Anicus Olybrius. With his son, Huneric, now married to the other daughter, Geiseric wanted Olybrius on the Western throne to cement his family alliance to the seat of West Roman power.

The last thing either Ricimer or Leo wanted at this time was to further strengthen the Vandal position. Quite probably, tied up in their negotiations was some sort of deal in which Constantinople got their man in Ravenna in return for once again helping the West against the Vandals. So it was that Anthemius, 'man of the eastern senate of great wealth and high birth' as Procopius says, became Western Emperor in 467. Anthemius had a good military record and brought Eastern troops with him when he arrived at Ravenna.

Geiseric was not happy with this and so, as Procopius again recounts: 'kept on plundering the whole land of the (Eastern) Emperor.'

'The Emperor Leo, wishing to punish the Vandals because of these things, was gathering an army against them; and they say that this army numbered 100,000 men. And he collected a fleet from the whole of the Mediterranean showing great generosity to both soldiers and sailors, for he feared lest from a parsimonious policy some obstacle might arise to hinder him in his desire to carry out his punishment of the barbarians.' (Procopius)

100,000 troops seems unlikely, unless this included ships' crews. When Belisarius sailed to Africa in 533, he had 500 ships carrying 10,000 foot soldiers and 5,000 cavalrymen with their horses. Crewing these 500 ships were 30,000 sailors (including rowers who, contrary to popular wisdom, were not slaves) and 2,000 marines. Leo's armada was no doubt larger. The number of 1,100 ships pops up again and even if this is not entirely reliable, the army it transported would have contained around 20,000 men, so something close to 1,000 ships is quite possible.

The cost of raising such a large amphibious invasion force was enormous, amounting to 130,000lb of gold according to several contemporary sources. To put this amount into perspective, Justinian's magnificent Saint Sophia basilica – the Hagia Sophia which still stands proudly over the Istanbul skyline today – cost 15-20,000lb of gold. Fortunately for the Vandals, the legacy of this much larger military expenditure was far shorter-lived.

The campaign started off badly for the Vandals. Marcellinus, commander of the Illyrian field army who had come west with Anthemius, drove the Vandals out of Sardinia. Meanwhile, another general, Heracleius, landed troops in Tripolitania to the east of Carthage where, according to Procopius, he easily defeated the Vandals in battle, 'Captured the cities and leaving his ships there, led his army on foot toward Carthage.'

Geiseric, however, was probably not overly perturbed by these defeats on the peripheries. He knew that the crunch would come at Carthage and, once again, he had no intention of conducting a passive defence. He had plenty of forewarning of the impending attack, so he gathered all the ships and the best seamen he could muster at Carthage, together with the cream of his army. Although the Roman fleet probably outnumbered his, Geiseric no doubt felt that if he could destroy the enemy at sea, the odds would be more in his favour than if he waited for an engagement on land.

The main Roman fleet, commanded by Basiliscus, probably first sailed to Sicily and, after re-provisioning, then set sail for Africa sometime in the summer of 468. Carthage was well protected and had a chain over the harbour so, rather than heading directly for the city, Basiliscus put in at a place called Mercurium, which Procopius says was 'no less than 280 stades' (60km) from Carthage. This was probably in the shelter of the western coast of the tip of Cap Bon, in modern Tunisia. At that time of year the prevailing winds are easterly, and that would have given the Roman fleet shelter as well as keeping the wind to their backs. No doubt the plan was to offload troops and then strike overland for Carthage, as the last thing the Romans wanted was a sea battle.

However, that is exactly what Geiseric gave them. Procopius writes: 'Arming all his subjects in the best way he [Geiseric] could, he filled his ships, but not all, for some he kept in readiness empty, and they were the ships which sailed most swiftly.'

Procopius tells us that Geiseric entered into negotiations with Basiliscus and, with a fair amount of gold, arranged a five-day truce in order to buy time to allow the wind to change, which did indeed happen. Now I am not sure how reliable the Vandal five-day weather forecast was back then, but if today's reports are anything to go on then betting everything on a certain wind change seems unlikely. What is more probable is that as the Romans were re-provisioning in Sicily, Geiseric did everything in his power to delay them in order to complete his own preparations. Then, with the Romans anchored off Mercurium, Geiseric seized the opportunity of the wind changing to a westerly in order to strike first.

'The Vandals, as soon as the wind had arisen for them which they had been expecting during the time they lay at rest, raised their sails and, taking in tow the boats which, as has been stated above, they had made ready with no men in them, they sailed against the enemy. And when they came near and their sails were bellied by the wind, they set fire to the boats which they were towing and let them go against the Roman fleet. And since there were a great number of ships there, these boats easily spread fire wherever they struck, and were themselves readily destroyed together with those with which they came into contact. And as the fire advanced in this way the Roman fleet was filled with tumult, as was natural. With a great din that rivalled the noise caused by the wind and the roaring of the flames, the soldiers and sailors shouted orders to one another and pushed the fire-boats off with their poles. They did the same with their own ships which were being destroyed by one another in complete disorder. Already the Vandals too were at hand ramming and sinking the ships and capturing those soldiers, together with their arms, who tried to escape.' (Procopius)

This is the first detailed description we have of any Vandal battle. Procopius, like the soldier-historian Ammianus Marcellinus in the fourth century, is a reliable source. Although he is recounting an event which took place half a century before his time, he had first hand experience of war against the Vandals and the sea voyage from Constantinople to Africa on board a Roman fleet. The Vandal tactics he describes are perfectly believable and echo those used by the English to break up the Spanish Armada in the sixteenth century. Geiseric's use of fire ships, taking advantage of a wind change and then swiftly followed up by a shock attack, show his genius as a military commander. Fire ships were not unknown in the ancient world, but there are no recorded instances of them being used during Geiseric's lifetime. He must have consulted Carthage's best sea captains for advice, and either he or his African-Roman advisors must have also delved into the archives. He could not have counted on a wind change so probably he had other plans up his sleeve as well. When the wind did change, he seized the opportunity without hesitation and dealt Rome a devastating blow.

It is worth continuing Procopius' account to the end as we rarely get such a close, near first hand account of a fifth century battle:

'There were also some attempts of the Romans who proved themselves brave men in the struggle. Most of all was John, who was one of Basiliscus' generals and who had no share in his treason. For a great throng having surrounded his ship, he stood on deck, and turning from side to side kept killing very great numbers of the enemy from there. When he perceived that the ship was being captured, he leapt with his whole equipment of arms from the deck into the sea. And though Genzon, son of Geiseric, entreated him earnestly not to do this, offering him pledges and holding out promises of safety, he nevertheless threw himself into the sea, uttering this one word, that John would never come under the hands of the dogs.'

This passage follows a long classical tradition of focusing on the heroic actions of one named man and blaming defeat on the treachery of the commanding general. What it does tell us is that after the fire-ships and the ramming there was vicious hand-to-hand fighting as the Vandals boarded some of the Roman ships. The story of John's heroic death is a personification of the actions of many unnamed Romans who probably bravely fought back and ended up in a watery grave. Procopius assigns treasonous motives to Basiliscus for not striking directly at Carthage and taking Vandal gold to give Geiseric time to act. He also suggests that the Aspar was behind the treason. Again this follows a well-trodden path. The defeat of a well-formed Roman force could not be put down to better intelligence, strategy and tactics by a mere barbarian. For Roman readers, a defeat of such enormous proportions could only be down to some treachery by disloyal Romans.

Procopius' account leaves a couple of unanswered questions. He implies that the Roman Army was onboard ship at the time the Vandals struck. If the fleet had indeed been at anchor, and maybe for a day or more, then it seems unlikely that all troops would have remained on board. Even in today's navies, the quality and spaciousness of onboard accommodation for foot soldiers leaves something to be desired and is never likely to get a good recommendation on TripAdvisor. Ancient transports and galleys were many times worse, with very little deck space and not even a place to sling a hammock. If Basiliscus' fleet had anchored off Mercurium for any length of time, then it is reasonable to assume that he would have begun to offload men, horses and supplies; especially if he had been intending to proceed overland from there, as indeed Belisarius did several years later. Perhaps the off-loading had begun and as the Vandal fleet hove into view, or possibly with advance warning of their approach, the soldiers were recalled to the ships to fight off the enemy.

Irritatingly, Procopius does not tell us what happened to the surviving ships and men. Some ships must have been able to break their way out, especially the *dromons* which were not dependent on wind alone. There must also have still been a substantial cadre of the army left on land. Procopius only says: 'So this war came to an end. Heracleius departed for home; for Marcellinus (in Sardinia) had been destroyed by one of his fellow officers.' We can only imagine the scattered ships limping back to Sicily and then Constantinople, leaving any men onshore to their fate. Basiliscus did make it back, seeking sanctuary in the Haiga Sophia from the Emperor's wrath. After Leo's death, he briefly became Emperor of the East.

The Battle of Mercurium, if we may call it that, was surely Geiseric's greatest single victory in open battle against Rome. It was also one of the most decisive battles of late antiquity. Yet, like so many of the Vandal achievements, it has gone virtually unremembered. Ask anyone, who knows something of the time, to name the most important battles of the late Roman Empire, and you will probably get Adrianople and Catalaunian Fields in response. The former was the victory of the Goths over the Romans in 378. It rewrote the script for Roman/barbarian interactions ever after and so it was indeed decisive. The second was Aeitus' defeat of Attila near Troyes in 451 and it was included in Sir Edward Creasy's *Fifteen Decisive Battles of the Western World*. It is true that Aetius checked the Huns and had the result been the other way around then the course of history may well have been changed. The result of Geiseric's victory over Basiliscus in 468 did in fact change history. It ended the West Roman Empire.

The combined forces of East and West Rome had staked all they had on a single throw of the dice, and the Vandals had won. The West, without Africa, was already bankrupt and now the East no longer had the means to come to their aid. Had the Romans won, then there is every chance the West Roman Empire could have recovered enough to hang on to part of western Europe in the same way as the Eastern Empire did over the near east for another millennium.

In the aftermath of the Vandal victory at Mercurium, the Visigoths, Franks and Burgundians flexed their muscles in Gaul, expanding their territories confident in the knowledge that there would be no new army coming from Italy to oppose them. The Visigoth King Euric even sent ambassadors to the Vandals seeking to bury the hatchet after years of enmity, realising that they were now a more important power than the rump of the Western Empire. Meanwhile, the *Baccaudae* in Gaul and Spain took matters into their own hands while the Britons had long ago been left to their own devices.

In Italy, Ricimer turned against Anthemius and had him killed in 472. Geiseric's son-in-law, Olybrius, was the next to be elevated to the increasingly crumbling throne, but by now its significance meant little. Olybrius and Ricimer both died shortly afterwards and the flurry of puppet emperors and new warlords that followed belong to another story. The reality was that after 468 the Western Empire no longer had the means to continue as a functioning state. For several more years she limped along on the prestige of her name, having no ability to pay the troops that claimed to serve her. In 476, Odovacar, the Scirian leader of the barbarian troops of the Italian army, decided that he had no need to rule in the name of an emperor any more and so did away with the fiction and ended the West Roman Empire forever. Had the Battle of Mercurium gone the other way, then the outcome would have been very different.

Geiseric lived on one more year after bringing about the collapse of the greatest empire the world has ever known. On his death bed, he made his family swear to a rather odd succession plan. Instead of the kingship passing to the eldest son, he insisted that it go to the oldest male of the family.

This seems a rather strange rule of succession and it caused his descendants more than a few family squabbles in later years. In all probability, Geiseric's motivation was based on his own experience. When his half-brother Gunderic died, Geiseric became king in preference to Gunderic's young sons, whom he later quietly did away with. This prevented leadership of the nascent Vandal-Alan coalition passing to a minor at a time when strong leadership was needed. Geiseric would also have been influenced by the problems caused when infant emperors ascended the Imperial throne, such as Valentinian II, Honorius and Valentinian III. Geiseric's will, therefore, ensured that this would not happen to the Vandals. It also legitimized his own ascension if he had been having any twinges of death-bed guilt. As Geiseric was in his late seventies or early eighties when he died, his son Huneric was already in his fifties when he became king. While ruling out child rulers in the future, the unintended consequence of Geiseric's will was that his successors were old men rather than young vigorous warriors. Over the next few generations of Vandal kings, this succession rule created as many problems as it solved.

Geiseric the Great?

Although very few people today would recognize his name, Geiseric deserves to be remembered as one of the greatest leaders of late antiquity. He managed to meld together several diverse groups of people into a single cohesive entity. Before he took the kingship, the Vandals had a pretty poor military record, yet Geiseric never lost a battle, even if he failed initially to take Hippo Regius and some of his forces were beaten when he was not personally present. He fought and defeated Suevi, Moors, West and East Romans by land. He led his people over thousands of miles of hostile territory; captured Carthage and Rome; and, having built up a navy from scratch, Geiseric took control of the Mediterranean and destroyed the huge East Roman invasion fleet at Mercurium, which sealed the fate of the Western Empire.

Geiseric came to power before either Aetius or Attila but he survived them both. He outlived and outwitted fourteen West Roman Emperors and five Eastern Emperors, as well as countless usurpers and powerful warlords. Above all, he held onto his conquests, while the West Roman Empire and the Empire of Attila both fell before Geiseric's death. Whenever a threat developed, Geiseric always struck first. He took Carthage by surprise in 439. He gathered his forces and sailed for Rome immediately after Valentinian III's murder, reaching the city long before the Romans could sort themselves out. When Majorian built a fleet in Spain, Geiseric sailed there and destroyed it before the Roman expedition got off the ground. Faced with a huge East Roman armada in 468, he used innovative tactics and exploited the weather to defeat it.

The fact that the Vandal Kingdom collapsed less than a century after he died does not in any way diminish his achievements. Although the creation of Vandal North Africa was no doubt largely down to Geiseric's personal leadership, the fact that it survived several generations of far less worthy kings shows that Geiseric had managed to create something more than a kingdom based on force of personality alone. By way of comparison, Attila's Hun Empire fell apart within a year of his death.

With hindsight, Geiseric's enthusiastic support of Arian Christianity, which kept Vandals and Romans apart, probably doomed the kingdom to eventual collapse. Only by integrating with their many more numerous subjects could Vandal North Africa hope to survive in the long term. Perhaps had he been more successful in converting his subjects to the Arian faith, just as the Arabs were with Islam in the seventh century, the Vandal Kingdom may have endured. However, adherence to the Catholic Nicene Creed was simply too strong and, as we shall see, the East Roman Empire was not yet a spent force.

Chapter 6

The Next Generation

In his fifties, Huneric became king of the Vandals and Alans in 477. His marriage to Eudocia had not lasted. Valentinian's daughter left Huneric in 472 and moved to Jerusalem, officially because of her Catholic faith and possibly as a result of a deal with the Eastern Empire in order for them to accept Olybrius on the Western throne without any difficult family ties to the Vandals.

To paraphrase Procopius: Huneric persecuted the Catholics, had trouble with the Moors and died of disease after ruling for eight years. He was succeeded by Gunthamund, his nephew, who was the next oldest male of the royal family. He too persecuted the Catholics, had more trouble with the Moors and died of disease after ruling for twelve years. The next Vandal king was Thrasamund, who was Gunthamund's brother, 'A man well favoured in appearance and especially gifted with discretion and high mindedness.' (Procopius)

Thrasamund took a different tack with his Catholic subjects, attempting conversion by persuasion rather than persecution. Despite ongoing difficulties with the Moors, when he ascended the throne in 496 the Vandals were still the most stable kingdom in the West and were incredibly wealthy. They occupied some of the most productive regions of the former West Roman Empire, their fleets controlled the Mediterranean and they had enriched themselves with the loot taken from Rome in 455. Elsewhere, Theodoric the Ostrogoth had moved into Italy, supplanted Odoacer and established a new kingdom. The Franks under Clovis had pushed the Visigoths out of Gaul and into Spain, while Anastasius was ruling the East Roman Empire.

Thrasamund sought an alliance with the Ostrogoths of Italy by marrying Amalafrida, Theodoric's sister. Her dowry included 5,000 Ostrogoth warriors and Lilybaeum in western Sicily. As well as securing the friendship of the Ostrogoths in Italy, Thrasamund made efforts to improve relations with the East Roman Empire. According to Procopius, he became 'a special friend' of the Emperor Anastasius: 'As a result of this Thrasamund was accounted the strongest and most powerful of all those who ruled over the Vandals.'

The Moors

In Geiseric's time the native North African Moors either served the Vandals as auxiliaries or kept out of the great king's way. 'For through fear of Geiseric the Moors had remained quiet at that time, but as soon as he was out of the way they both did much harm to the Vandals and suffered the same themselves.' (Procopius)

Like some of their Berber descendants today, the Moors lived on the periphery of the settled agricultural regions of North Africa, leading a nomadic lifestyle which endured while civilized empires rose and fell. They had fought for and against Hannibal, Scipio and Julius Caesar. Their light cavalry are depicted on Trajan's Column in Rome fighting as auxiliaries, and the *Notitia Dignitatum* lists many units of *Mauri* serving in all parts of the Roman Empire. They were famous for their light cavalry – expert horsemen who would use agility and speed to shower the enemy with javelins while keeping out of harm's way from more heavily-equipped troops such as the Vandals and Romans. They also employed large numbers of similarly lightly-equipped men on foot. They too would have been primarily javelin-armed skirmishers who could support the horsemen. Tough, nimble and fleet of foot, they could also move with ease over the rough mountain terrain that formed the southern borders of Vandal North Africa.

> 'Horses and men were tiny and gaunt; the riders unequipped and unarmed, except that they carried javelins with them; the horses without bridles, their very motion being the ugly gait of animals running with stiff necks and outstretched heads.' (Livy)

Although this passage was written many years previously the Moors do not appear to have changed much over the succeeding years. Procopius, writing eight centuries later, is at pains to show their hardiness, describing a way of eating grain that sounds not dissimilar to modern North African couscous:

'The Moors live in stuffy huts both in winter and in summer.... And they sleep on the ground, the prosperous among them, if it should so happen, spreading a fleece under themselves.... And they have neither bread nor wine nor any other good thing, but they take grain, either wheat or barley and, without boiling it or grinding it to flour or barley-meal, they eat it in a manner not a whit different from that of the animals.'

As we have already seen, Vandal tactics, favouring hand-to-hand combat exclusively, were the complete opposite of the Moors. Knowledge of horse archery, that some of their Alan ancestors would have had in the fourth century, had long been forgotten. In the early-fifth century many or most Vandals would have fought on foot. As horses became more available, they increasingly took to mounted combat although, in their early years, they may still have dismounted when the circumstances suited it. After the establishment of their African kingdom, every Vandal warrior had the means to own and train good cavalry mounts and so took to fighting on horseback exclusively. The Vandals had no response to the fast hit-and-run attacks of the Moors, who would retreat to mountain strongholds when faced by a stronger enemy. As a result the Vandals often found themselves at a loss when trying to deal with the incursions, which happened with increasing frequency after Geiseric's death.

Already during Huneric's reign, the Moors began to chip away at the peripheries of the Vandal Kingdom. One group of Moors occupied Mount Aurasium (Jebel Auress in the Aurès region of modern Algeria) and used it as a secure refuge from which to raid the fertile plains to the north east. The Vandals were unable to do anything about them, as by the time any Vandal troops arrived the Moors melted back into the mountains, where steep slopes and difficult access made pursuit impossible for the Vandal heavy cavalry. As a result the Aurès Mountains, only thirteen days' travel west from Carthage, remained a Moorish stronghold well beyond the end of the Vandal Kingdom. Many centuries later, the Moors' Berber descendants used this same area as a guerrilla base against the French during the Algerian War of Independence.

There were numerous small clans of Moors, all of whom operated independently under their own leaders. Spread out over thousands of kilometres of harsh mountain and desert terrain, they operated as small bands rather than uniting as a single nation. A Latin inscription dated to the early part of Huneric's reign records the independence of the Moors of the Aurès Mountains and a lingering adherence to Roman rather than Vandal authority:

'I Masties, Duke for sixty-seven years and Emperor for ten years, never perjured myself nor broke faith with either Romans or the Moors, and was prepared in both war and in peace, and my deeds were such that God supported me well.'

Further west, another Latin inscription from 508 commemorates the building of a fort by Masuna, King of the Moors and Romans. Again no mention is made of the Vandals.

During Thrasamund's reign, the Moorish leader, Cabon, caused the Vandals trouble in Tripolitania (the western coastal region of modern Libya). Procopius gives a detailed description of a campaign which highlights some of the difficulties the Vandals had in dealing with the Moors. Cabon exploited the division between the Arian Vandal overlords and their Catholic Roman subjects. He treated Catholic churches with reverence, while the Vandals did the opposite. The highly mobile Moors kept the Vandal army under constant observation when they marched east from Carthage to oppose them.

'The Vandals, upon making camp the first day, led their horses and their other animals into the temples of the [Catholic] Christians, and sparing no insult they acted with all the unrestrained lawlessness natural to them, beating as many priests as they caught and lashing them with many blows over the back and commanding them to render such service to the Vandals as they were accustomed to assign to the most dishonoured of their domestics. And as soon as they had departed from there, the spies of Cabon did as they had been directed to do; for straightaway they cleansed the sanctuaries and took away with great care the filth and whatever other unholy things lay in them... and after giving pieces of silver to the poor who sat about

these sanctuaries, they then followed after the army of the Vandals.'
(Procopius)

This passage shows that the ancient Moors understood the importance of
winning the 'hearts and minds' of the local populace in the same way as
successful insurgent groups still do today. But Cabon did not only fight
a guerrilla war against the Vandals. He also stood up to them in battle
using some novel tactics, as Procopius recounts:

'He [Cabon] marked off a circle in the plain where he was about to
make a palisade, and placed his camels turned sideways in a circle as
a protection for the camp, making his line fronting the enemy about
twelve camels deep. Then he placed the women and children and all
those who were unfit for fighting together with their possessions in
the middle, while he commanded the host of fighting men to stand
between the feet of those animals and cover themselves with their
shields.... The Vandals were at a loss how to handle the situation; for
they were neither good with the javelin nor with the bow, nor did they
know how to go into battle on foot, but they were all horsemen, and
used spears and swords for the most part, so that they were unable to
do the enemy any harm at a distance; and their horses, annoyed at the
sight of the camels, refused absolutely to be driven against the enemy.
And since the Moors, by hurling javelins in great numbers among
them from their safe position, kept killing both their horses and men
without difficulty, because they were a vast throng. They [the Vandals]
began to flee and when the Moors came up against them, the most of
them were destroyed while some fell into the hands of the enemy and
an exceedingly small number of the army returned home. Such was
the fortune which Thrasamund suffered at the hands of the Moors.'

By the end of Thrasamund's reign, most of the Mauretanias in the
west, a large part of southern Numidia, as well as enclaves in Byzacena
and Tripolitania were under Moorish rather than Vandal control. The
latter increasingly concentrated close to Carthage, their numbers too
small to control the thousands of kilometres of frontier bordering the
less prosperous regions. As there was no single Moorish nation, not
all bands were hostile. Many found it more profitable to trade with the

Vandals and take service in their armies rather than raiding them. Right to the very end of the Vandal Kingdom there were Moors fighting in the Vandal army.

Life in Vandal Africa

The Vandals who followed Godegisel and then Geiseric from the forests of central Europe through Gaul, Spain and North Africa, experienced a life of unimaginable hardship. Only the very toughest would have survived the more than two decades it took before they finally had a home they could call their own. Another two decades on and they were masters of the richest province of the West Roman Empire. They ruled the Mediterranean and decorated the villas they had appropriated from the African-Roman aristocrats with all the portable loot that Rome had amassed over the preceding millennium.

Like the modern baby-boomers enjoying the prosperity of the 1950s/60s after their parents' sacrifices in the Depression and Second World War, the children and grandchildren of Geiseric's generation took to the good life with a vengeance. Living on grand prosperous estates worked by armies of slaves and poorer subject Romans – and with the tedious bureaucracy of government being left to better-off Romans – a life of luxury would have been hard to resist, as Procopius describes:

'For all the nations which we know, that of the Vandals is the most luxurious and that of the Moors the most hardy. For the Vandals, since the time when they gained possession of Libya, used to indulge in baths, all of them, every day, and enjoyed a table abounding in all things, the sweetest and best that earth and sea produce. And they wore gold very generally, and clothed themselves in the Medic garments which they now call silk, and passed their time, thus dressed, in hippodromes and in other pleasurable pursuits, and above all else in hunting. And they had dancers and mimes and all other things to hear and see which are of a musical nature or otherwise merit attention among men. And the most of them dwelt in parks, which were well supplied with water and trees; and they had great numbers of banquets, and all manner of sexual pleasures were in great vogue amongst them.'

The late-fifth century Roman rhetorician, Malchus, gives a similar verdict on the post-Geiseric generation:

'After the death of Geiseric they had fallen completely into softness and had maintained neither the same strength for action nor had the same military establishment which he had kept ready for use, so that he [Geiseric] always moved more quickly than his opponents calculated.'

Always on the outlook to prove the perils of moral degeneracy, nineteenth century Europeans were quick to latch onto such passages to explain the relatively rapid collapse of the Vandal Kingdom in 533. Unsurprisingly, since the 1960s, modern historians have rejected this as too simplistic. However, it is not difficult to see why the succeeding generations of Vandals would have embraced the good life after so many years of hardship. Geiseric had to fight an offensive campaign against all comers in order to establish a homeland. His descendants had no desire to expand their kingdom, only to hold onto it and enjoy the 'peace dividend'. This does not necessarily mean that the Vandal warriors of the sixth century were weaker or more degenerate than their forefathers, any more than modern British soldiers in Afghanistan are any less valiant that their ancestors on the Somme or at El Alamein. The experience of the Vandal army of the sixth century was in fighting Moorish insurgents and, unlike Geiseric's men, they never had to face a well-organized, well-equipped and well-supplied conventional opponent.

With only a small number of Vandals controlling a vast area, with a much larger number of disaffected Roman subjects and hostile Moors picking away at the outlying regions, it is not surprising that the kingdom could not survive every concerted effort to destroy it. Each Vandal warrior killed in battle was hard to replace, while the Moors and the East Romans could afford casualties. The uncoordinated bands of Moors would never have the strength to take over the Vandal Kingdom, although they could whittle away at the periphery. Against the Romans, the Vandals had to win every single battle while the Romans could absorb a loss and come back another day when circumstances changed. Under Geiseric, the Vandals had survived many attempts to destroy them but it was probably only a matter of time before the inevitable happened. It will always be an uneven fight when you need to win every single battle while your opponent only needs to win one.

The King, The Queen, and The Usurper

Thrasamund died on 6 May 523. His successor was Hilderic, son of Huneric and Eudocia. As the oldest male of the royal line, Hilderic was the grandson of both Geiseric and Valentinian III. He was probably between 50 and 60 years of age at the time of his coronation and would have had a reasonable claim to the West Roman throne had the Empire survived. No doubt due to his mother's influence, Hilderic adopted a pro-Roman and pro-Catholic policy. He allowed Catholic bishops to return to the Vandal Kingdom, reopened churches that had been closed by his predecessors and maintained friendly relations with the East Roman Empire.

Needless to say, this did not go down well with the fiercely Arian Vandal nobility, and many of them turned to Amalafrida, Thrasamund's Ostrogothic widow, to be their champion. In 525, civil war broke out with the disaffected Vandal nobles allying with Amalafrida's Ostrogoths and calling in some Moors to help them. A battle was fought at Caspa, 300 miles south of Carthage. We have no details of what occurred other than the fact that the Hilderic was victorious. He imprisoned Amalafrida at Carthage and executed the survivors of her Ostrogoth bodyguard. This led Theodoric, the Ostrogoth King, to contemplate an amphibious invasion of Vandal Africa. His death in 526 put an end to the plan. Hilderic kept Amalafrida alive while her brother was still living, but when Theodoric died he had her executed.

According to Procopius, Hilderic was no warrior. He wanted nothing to do with the unpleasant business of fighting the Moors to defend the Vandal Kingdom, preferring to leave this to his young nephew, Hoamer. In the late 520s the Moorish chieftain Antalas started raiding into Byzacena. Hoamer pushed him back into the mountains but failed to dislodge him. The Moors then attacked the Vandals when they were resupplying and soundly defeated them.

A Germanic king was supposed to be his people's pre-eminent war leader and Hilderic had abdicated this responsibility. Furthermore, having done so, his army had been defeated. Whatever simmering

disquiet had been suppressed with Amalafrida's defeat now again rose
to the surface. Next in line to the Vandal throne, according to Geiseric's
law of succession, was Gelimer. He was Geiseric's great-grandson, son
of Geilaris – Thrasamund's younger brother.

> 'This man [Gelimer] was thought to be the best warrior of his time, but
> for the rest he was a cunning fellow and base of heart and well versed
> in undertaking revolutionary enterprises and laying his hands on the
> money of others.... He was no longer able to restrain his thoughts,
> but allying himself with all the noblest of the Vandals, he persuaded
> them to wrest the kingdom from Hilderic, as being an unwarlike king
> who had been defeated by the Moors.... Thus Gelimer seized the
> supreme power and imprisoned Hilderic, and also Hoamer and his
> brother Hoageis, after he [Hilderic] had ruled the Vandals for seven
> years.' (Procopius)

Gelimer, therefore, became King of the Vandals and Alans on 15 June
530. He was supported by the vast majority of the Vandal nobles, who
had become disenchanted by Hilderic's unwarlike ways and pro-Roman
tendencies. Hilderic had become very friendly with the new East
Roman Emperor Justinian. No doubt the prospect of a more malleable
Vandal regime and the possible restoration of the Catholic Church in
North Africa had been welcomed by the Romans. Now, with Gelimer's
usurpation, such hopes were dashed.

Procopius tells us of furious diplomatic messages being sent back and
forth between Constantinople and Carthage, with the Emperor Justinian
telling Gelimer to wait for his turn at the kingship until Hilderic's
natural death and Gelimer replying that Hilderic was planning to change
Geiseric's succession law to give the kingship to his closest relatives rather
than the oldest male of the line. Gelimer had Hoamer blinded, which
ruled out him ever becoming king, and he refused repeated requests
from Justinian to send Hilderic, Hoamer and Hoageis to Constantinople.
Procopius reports Gelimer's response to Justinian's diplomatic notes as
follows:

> 'King Gelimer to the Emperor Justinian. Neither have I taken the
> office by violence nor has anything unholy been done by me to my

kinsmen. For Hilderic, while planning a revolution against the house of Geiseric, was dethroned by the nation of the Vandals. I was called to my kingdom by my years, which gave me preference according to the law. Now it is well for one to administer the kingly office which belongs to him and not to make the concerns of others his own. Hence for you also, who have a kingdom, meddling in other's affairs is not just; and if you break the treaty and come against us, we shall oppose you with all our power, calling to witness the oaths which were sworn by Zeno, from whom you have received the kingdom which you hold.'

If Justinian had already been angry with Gelimer, the Vandal king's effrontery in presenting himself as an equal to the East Roman Emperor added insult to injury. Gelimer's timing was bad. Justinian had only ascended to the throne in 527. He was young, energetic and had just concluded a reasonably successful war against the Persians. By 533, the East Roman Empire's frontiers were secure, riots in Constantinople had been suppressed and the Roman Army was led by the rising star Belisarius, who had won victory against the Persians and put down the riots with a brutal efficiency. Greek was replacing Latin as the principal language of the Eastern Empire, but Justinian was a native Latin speaker who looked to the West and dreamed of re-establishing Rome's ancient glories.

Thus the stage was set for the confrontation to come.

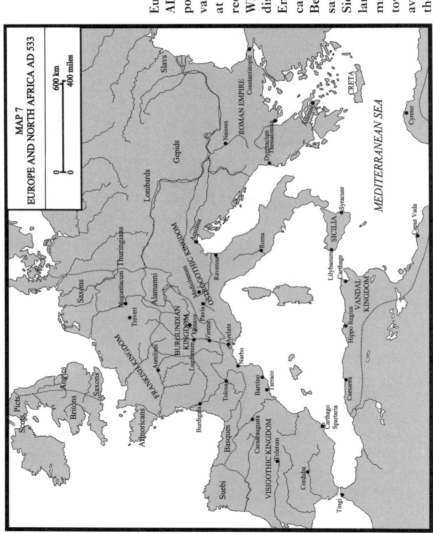

Europe and North Africa AD 533. This map shows the political boundaries of the various barbarian kingdoms at the time of the Vandal Africa. While the Western Empire reconquest of Vandal Africa. While the Western Empire disappeared in 476, the Eastern Empire continued with its capital at Constantinople. Belisarius' invasion force sailed from Constantinople to Sicily and, after replenishing, landed at Caput Vada. They made their way overland towards Carthage in order to avoid a naval engagement with the Vandals.

Chapter 7

The Empire Strikes Back

Justinian's Plans and Gelimer's Troubles

'In the seventh year of Justinian's reign [AD 533], at about the spring equinox, the Emperor commanded the general's [Belisarius'] ship to anchor off the point which is before the royal palace. Thither came also Epiphanus, the patriarch of Constantinople.... And after this the general Belisarius, and Antonia, his wife, set sail. And there was also with them Procopius, who wrote this history.... And the whole fleet followed the general's ship and they put in at Perinthus [Eregli on the Sea of Marmora] where five days were spent by the army, since at that place the general received as a present from the Emperor an exceedingly great number of horses from the royal pastures, which are kept for him in Thrace.' (Procopius)

So it was that, for the fourth time, a great Roman invasion fleet set sail to wrest control of Africa from the Vandals. We have only scant details of the previous Roman attempts at amphibious invasion in 441, 460 and 468, but we are fortunate that Procopius actually accompanied Belisarius in 533 and that his histories have survived intact. He gives us full details of the fleet and army which set sail from Constantinople in the spring of 533, which included:

500 transport ships with 30,000 sailors;
92 Dromons with 2,000 rowers who doubled as marines;
10,000 Roman infantry;
5,000 Roman cavalry;
400 Herul cavalry; and
600 Hun cavalry.

If the previous accounts are correct, which give 1,100 ships for the failed invasions of 441 and 468, then Justinian must have been feeling quite optimistic to attempt it with half that number. Also 16,000 soldiers seems like a rather small army to attack a well-established kingdom which could probably muster at least 20,000 warriors. The numbers that Procopius gives are, however, probably far more believable than most estimates we get of ancient armies. First of all he was actually there and, as Belisarius' secretary, he would have had access to the loading manifests and logistical arrangements – maybe even having a hand in drawing them up. Keeping an army supplied in the field is often what decides the success or failure of a campaign. This would have been the prime consideration in maintaining an army in Africa, thousands of miles away from home and with little chance of resupply. Once the Roman force landed they would have to live off the land, and therefore had a greater chance of success if it was composed of a relatively small number of picked troops rather than being padded out with more men and horses of lesser quality.

Needless to say, given the previous disastrous attempts against the Vandals, there were many in the court at Constantinople who tried to dissuade Justinian from his dream of reconquest. The cost would be enormous and the outcome doubtful. Just as today when a government is elected and fresh-faced ministers enthuse about their grand plans for the future, the senior civil servants suck in their breath and do their best to tell the minister that it has been tried before, did not work then and is unlikely to work now. It is not difficult to imagine the scene as Justinian gathered his advisors and told them that he wanted them to finance a fleet and army to retake Africa. One can only sympathize with John the Cappadocian who, as Praetorian Prefect, had to work out where the money would come from. Procopius tells us that while most other advisors kept their doubts to themselves, John, 'A man of great daring and the cleverest of all men of his time', dared to speak out.

After praising the Emperor's wisdom and professing his great loyalty, Procopius reports that John said that if Justinian had confidence he could vanquish the Vandals, even if the struggle was prolonged, then no doubt he would prevail and the cost in blood and treasure would be worth it.' For victory, coming at the end, covers up all the calamities of war.' John then continued:

'You are proposing to make an expedition against Carthage, to which, if he goes by land, the journey is of 140 days, and if one goes by water, he is forced to cross the whole open sea and go to its very end. So he who brings you news of what happens there will take a year after the event to reach you. And one might add that you could not take Libya while Sicily and Italy lie in the hands of others [the Ostrogoths]. If any reverse should befall you, Oh Emperor, the treaty having been broken by you will bring danger to our own lands. In a word, it will not be possible for you to reap the fruits of victory and at the same time any reversal of fortune will bring harm to what we have well established.'

Apparently Justinian saw the wisdom in John's advice, which neatly summed up the strategic difficulties. To succeed, the Romans would need a secure base close to Carthage, and even then conducting an amphibious invasion so far from home was fraught with danger. In many ways the course of action Justinian was considering was not unlike that which Margaret Thatcher proposed in 1982 to retake the Falklands. It involved sending a fleet far from home, landing a small task force to take on superior numbers and counting on the support of the local population. The distance between Constantinople and Carthage was much less than that between London and Port Stanley, but the Romans did not have the benefit of modern communications or aircraft.

An unnamed bishop then told Justinian that he had a dream in which God had pointed out that the Emperor had a duty to protect the African Catholics against the Vandal persecutions. God himself would join him in the war to free Africa from the Vandals. Procopius tells us that this was what eventually persuaded Justinian to stay the course, but there were other events which probably helped.

The first of these was a revolt of local Romans against Vandal rule in Tripolitania (the modern Libyan coast). No doubt encouraged by the hostility between Constantinople and Carthage, the African-Roman Pudentius led a rebellion against the Vandal overlords and asked Justinian for support. According to Procopius, Justinian sent an officer by the name of Tattimuth, clearly of Germanic origin, and 'an army of no great size' to bolster the Roman rebels. They were successful in wresting Tripolitania from the Vandals because Gelimer was otherwise occupied.

Godas, the Vandal governor of Sardinia, had risen in revolt. Godas was a Goth, possibly one of those who had previously served Queen Amalafrida and who escaped Hilderic's purge, but we do not know this for certain. Procopius says that he was 'passionate and energetic... well-disposed to the cause of his [Vandal] master.' However that may have been, Godas sniffed the changing winds and decided to take Sardinia for himself and approach Justinian for aid. He sent a message to Constantinople and asked for Roman support. Justinian saw this as an opportunity to get a secure base closer to Carthage and sent an envoy, Eulogius, to work out a deal with Godas to support him in return for his allegiance. Justinian also made ready 400 soldiers under Cyrus to aid the Goth-Vandal rebel. This was more than Godas was willing to accept. He had already started to style himself as a king and was no more inclined to accept Justinian as his master than he was to keep Gelimer. Even if Godas' revolt did not give Sardinia to Justinian on a plate, it did distract Gelimer, as Procopius recounts:

'Gelimer, being deprived of Tripolitania by Prudentius and of Sardinia by Godas, scarcely hoped to regain Tripolitania, since it was situated at a great distance and the rebels were already being assisted by the Romans, against whom just at that moment it seemed to him best not to take the field. But he was eager to take the island before an army sent by the Emperor to fight for his enemies should arrive there. He accordingly selected 5,000 of the Vandals and 120 ships of the fastest kind, and appointing as general his brother Tzazon, he sent them off.'

So it was that just as Justinian was preparing his invasion fleet, Gelimer sent off the better part of his, along with 5,000 troops, to retake Sardinia. If Gelimer had known Justinian's intentions, he surely would not have done this. He could not have been unaware that the Romans were amassing a fleet at Constantinople, but probably thought that their intention was to take Sardinia rather than attack Carthage. There are some hints that Justinian carried out a deception plan. Belisarius was recalled from the eastern frontier after the conclusion of the Persian war in 532 without any announcement, even to Belisarius himself. A story was given out that the general had been removed from office and recalled in disgrace in order to hide the real reason. Justinian had sent troops to aid Prudentius in Tripolitania and was openly negotiating with Godas. Gelimer probably assumed that the Roman fleet's destination was Sardinia, so he sent his ships there.

Sicily was a vital base for the success of an expedition against Carthage. Only a day's sail away, it was the perfect safe harbour and supply base. All of the previous Roman expeditions against the Vandals had used Sicily as their jumping-off point, but then Sicily had been under Roman control. Now it was part of the Ostrogoth Kingdom of Italy. The Ostrogoths, however, were not best pleased with the Vandals in the aftermath of Amalafrida's execution. The Ostrogoths were at this time being ruled by Amalasuntha, Theodoric's daughter and Amalafrida's niece. She ran the Kingdom of Italy as regent for her infant son, Athalaric. When Justinian's envoys approached her, she was more than happy to provide a supply base in Sicily for a Roman force which would avenge Amalafrida's death.

So it was that the political and strategic situation favoured the Romans rather that the Vandals for the first time in over 100 years.

Belisarius' Army

The Roman Army had changed and evolved from that which Godegisel and Geiseric had fought in the fifth century. Just as it had been with the Vandals, cavalry had become the most important part of the Roman Army. Although infantry still formed the largest contingent in Belisarius' force they were no longer the decisive arm. The role of the infantry was to hold ground and garrison towns while the cavalry delivered the decisive blow.

The Roman cavalry had also evolved. In the fifth century, most Roman cavalrymen were armed with spears and javelins. Under the influence of the Huns and Persians, horse archery had been increasingly adopted by the Romans. Most of Belisarius' cavalry were bow-armed but they were not lightly-equipped skirmishers. Wearing body armour of mail or scale and equipped with good swords, they were perfectly happy closing into hand-to-hand combat as well as shooting arrows from a distance. Some also carried spears in addition to their bows and swords, but probably not all of them.

Procopius describes the Roman cavalry of his day:

'The bowmen of the present time go into battle wearing corselets and fitted out with greaves [leg protectors] which extend up to the knee. From the right hand side hang their arrows, from the other a sword. And there are those who have a spear also attached to them, and at the shoulders a sort of small shield without a grip, such as to cover the region of the face and neck. They are expert horsemen and are able without difficulty to direct their bows to either side while riding at full speed, and to shoot at an opponent whether in pursuit or flight. They draw the bowstring along by the forehead about opposite the right ear, thereby discharging the arrow with such an impetus as to kill whoever stands in the way shield and corselet alike having no power to check its force.'

The later sixth century military manual, the *Strategikon*, describes the training exercises carried out by the Roman cavalryman of the time to enable him to use both missile and shock tactics:

'On horseback at a run, he should fire one or two arrows rapidly and put the strung bow in its case. Then he should grab the spear which he has been carrying on his back. With the strung bow in its case, he should hold the spear in his hand, then quickly replace it on his back and grab the bow.'

This made the Roman cavalryman of 533 someone who could either fight from a distance or close into combat. He could ride up to his opponents, shower them with arrows, retreat out of harm's way and then suddenly turn back to attack with spear or sword. He was supplemented in Belisarius' army by 400 Heruls, unarmoured Germans who fought hand-to-hand only, and 600 Hun light horse archers, whom Procopius calls Massagetae. Also amongst those classified by Procopius as regular Roman cavalry were the *foederati*. Initially this term was applied to barbarians in Roman service, but by 533 the terminology remained even if the reality had changed.

'Now at an earlier time the only barbarians had been enlisted amongst the *foederati*... but at the present time there is nothing to prevent anyone from assuming the name, since time will by no means consent to keep names attached to the things to which they were formerly applied.' (Procopius)

Just as a man serving in a regiment of light cavalry in today's British Army is neither light nor a horseman, a trooper in a regiment of *foederati* in the sixth century Roman Army was not necessarily a barbarian in the way that a fourth or fifth century Roman would have understood the term. It may be that the *foederati* were spear and shield-armed cavalry of the same type as the majority of the Vandals, in contrast to the bow-armed regular cavalry and Huns.

Belisarius also had with him 1,100 of his own *bucellarii*, men who were his personal troops. These men are referred to variously as *doruphoroi* (spear bearers) and *hypapsistai* (shield bearers). The former appear to have been a sort of inner guard who also acted as staff officers, while the latter were elite cavalrymen. All were probably very well-equipped mounted warriors with body armour, bows, spears, swords and shields. They owed their loyalty to the general personally and were maintained by him rather than by the state.

Roman infantry were the largest part of Belisarius' army, but they took little part in his set piece battles against the Vandals. Their role was to hold ground, provide a secure rallying point for the cavalry, guard the baggage and garrison any towns captured along the way. They were typically a mix of spearmen and archers, with the former deployed in the front ranks forming a phalanx and protected by large oval shields, the latter shooting overhead from behind. Typically, the archers accounted for about a quarter of the infantry.

Gelimer's Army

In contrast to the Romans, Gelimer did not have a combined arms force. Any problems the Vandals may have had with securing good cavalry mounts in the migration years would have long been overcome. Like the knights of medieval Europe, each Vandal warrior was in effect an aristocrat, maintained on a large estate worked by subject Romans. Apart from enjoying life as a conquerer, the only real occupation for a Vandal man was to be a warrior. He probably had a string of good horses and was very well equipped with helmet, body armour, shield, sword and spear.

With the riches of North Africa at their disposal, not to mention the loot gathered from the sack of Rome and their pirate raids, none of Gelimer's followers would have gone lacking. Herein lay a problem. The Romans were excluded from the army and there was no mass of Vandal peasant farmers to provide foot soldiers or archers to support the well-equipped mounted warriors. Gelimer could call on small numbers of lightly-equipped Moors to provide some balance to his force but, as we have seen, relations with the Moors had deteriorated to the point that most were now hostile. Those who were not chose to sit on the fence to see how things worked out rather than throwing their undivided support behind Gelimer.

Therefore the Vandal Army of 533 consisted almost exclusively of heavy cavalry who had one tactic only. That was to charge the enemy and engage them in hand-to-hand combat. Such a charge could be devastating. The *Strategikon* describes it, advising spear-armed Roman cavalry to adopt their methods of fighting:

'They [the front ranks] then lean forward, cover their heads with their shields, hold their lances high as their shoulders in the manner of the fair-haired races, and protected by their shields they ride in good order, not too fast but at a trot, to avoid having the impetus of the charge breaking up their ranks before coming to blows with the enemy, which is a real risk.'

In generic descriptions of Germanic tactics, the *Strategikon* notes that they were less likely than Romans to pay attention to keeping order in the ranks.

'The light haired races place great value on freedom. They are bold and undaunted in battle. Daring and impetuous as they are, they consider any timidity and even a short retreat as a disgrace. They calmly despise death as they fight violently in hand to hand combat.... They are undisciplined in charging, as if they were the only people in the world who are not cowards.'

With such a limited tactical repertoire and without light troops or infantry, the Vandals were vulnerable to skirmish tactics, ambushes, feints and flank attacks. If they charged the Roman horse archers, the latter could withdraw towards their secure infantry base, shooting arrows as they went. Then, when the Vandal horses tired and their ranks had broken up, the Roman cavalry could turn around and defeat them in close combat.

We really have no idea how many warriors Gelimer could call on. A century after the 80,000 Vandals crossed the Straits of Gibraltar, it is reasonable to assume that they had grown in number, especially as they had experienced many years of relative peace and prosperity. Procopius says as much: 'By their natural increase and by associating with other barbarians they came to be an exceedingly numerous people.' Maybe Gelimer had something like 30,000 warriors under his command, but it would not have been possible for him to bring them all together in a single army. Garrisons would have to be left behind, some would be needed to guard the frontiers against the Moors and, as we have seen, 5,000 had been sent to Sardinia to deal with Godas' revolt.

In many ways the situation of 406 had been reversed. Then, the more numerous Romans were unable to marshal enough troops to prevent the Rhine crossing. Now a relatively small Roman Army was on its way to Africa with one single objective. Meanwhile, Gelimer had to spread his forces to deal with a several simultaneous threats.

The Opening Moves

It was not all plain sailing for the Romans. Almost immediately Belisarius had to deal with disciplinary problems. When the fleet was laid up for four days because of lack of wind, two Huns killed one of their fellows in a drunken brawl. Belisarius impaled the miscreants, almost inciting a mutiny in the process. Then there were also serious supply problems. First of all the bread, that was supposed to be hard baked to last the voyage, had not been properly double baked. It dissolved into mouldy flour, resulting in the deaths of 500 men from food poisoning. According to Procopius this was down to cost-cutting measures implemented by John the Cappadocian to save on firewood. Plagued by gentle winds, the fleet took longer to reach Sicily than anticipated and as a result the water also spoiled.

Keeping a large fleet together was no easy matter. Procopius says that Belisarius was worried that if high winds came up the fleet might be scattered. His solution was to paint part of the three lead ships red and hang lights on them, so if any ships should lose their way they could easily see where they needed to sail to rejoin the fleet. As a result no ships were lost in the long voyage to Sicily.

The next problem was fear of the Vandal fleet itself. This became a major factor once the Romans reached Sicily. Belisarius had little intelligence of the Vandal dispositions and was apparently unaware that their fleet had gone to Sardinia to deal with Godas. The Romans had no experience of fighting at sea and were well aware that the Vandals had destroyed the previous invasion fleet in 468.

'[Belisarius was] disturbed by the soldiers who were in mortal dread of sea fighting and had no shame in saying beforehand that if they should be disembarked on land they would try to show themselves brave men, but if hostile ships assailed them, they would turn to flight. They said that they were not able to contend against two enemies at once, both men and water.' (Procopius)

Procopius himself was sent to Syracuse to seek news of the Vandal fleet before Belisarius attempted to cross over to Africa. Here Procopius met a man 'who had been a fellow citizen and friend of his from childhood, who had been living in Syracuse for a long time engaged in the shipping business. Here he learned what he wanted.' The news was that the Vandals had no idea of the Roman movements, that their fleet was at Sardinia and that Gelimer himself was staying at Hermione, four days inland from Carthage. With this news Belisarius set sail. Procopius says: 'A strong east wind arose for them and on the following day it carried the ships to the point off Libya at the place the Romans call "Caput Vada" or "Shoal's Head".' This place, Chebba in modern Tunisia, is 130 miles to the east of Carthage. The Romans made landfall there three months after their departure from Constantinople.

On landing, Belisarius called his commanders together to discuss the best course of action. There were two viable options. One was to strike immediately for Carthage. This was proposed by Archelaus, one of Belisarius' senior commanders, who felt that a long overland land march over arid land in midsummer, with all the attendant supply problems, might well end in disaster. Furthermore, with no walled towns along the way, thanks to Geiseric's dismantling of such defences, there would be no secure bases. Belisarius, on the other hand, judged that as they had already safely landed without a sea battle he did not want to risk the fate that befell the 468 expedition and suddenly find himself engaged by Vandal ships. The army could march along the coast, with the ships following within sight so as to help with resupply.

Needless to say, the general's opinion held the day. Procopius records his orders:

'We must disembark with all possible speed, landing horses and arms and whatever else we consider necessary for our use. We must dig a trench quickly and throw up a stockade around us of a kind which can contribute to our safety no less that a walled town one might mention. With that as our base we must carry on the war from there if anyone should attack us.'

Like Cabon the Moor before him, Belisarius was careful to treat the local population well, so that the Roman Army would be seen as liberators rather than conquerors. Even to the Vandals he presented himself as someone who had come to rid them of a usurper in support of Hilderic, 'their rightful king'. When some of the Roman soldiers 'went out into the fields and laid hands on the fruit there, the general inflicted corporal punishment of no casual sort on them,' according to Procopius. In a speech to his men, Belisarius pressed on them the need to keep the native Roman-Africans on side, to treat them as allies and pay for all provisions.

The Romans marched towards Carthage with an advance guard of 300 *bucellarii* led by John the Armenian about 4km in front of the main body. Their right flank was guarded by the sea and the ships that followed the army's progress. The open country to the left was the most dangerous, and to protect that flank Belisarius sent out the 600 light mobile Hun horse archers with orders to patrol at a distance of more than 4km from the main column. The Romans took Syllectus, a day's march from their landing place, where the local inhabitants supplied them with food and supplies. Then after passing Hadrumentum (Sousse in modern Tunisia), the Romans made camp at Grasse (Sidi Khalifa), where they availed themselves of the riches of one of Gelimer's royal estates.

Procopius' description of Grasse gives us some further insight into the life of wealth and luxury enjoyed by the Vandal nobles, which is also attested in surviving mosaics from that time:

'In that place was a palace of the ruler of the Vandals and a park, the most beautiful of all we know. For it is excellently watered by springs and has a great wealth of woods. And all the trees are full of fruit; so that each one of the soldiers pitched his tent among the fruit-trees, and though all of them ate their fill of the fruit, which was then ripe, there was practically no diminution of it.'

Gelimer's Response

Unfortunately we have no Vandal historian to give us the similar sort of detail for Gelimer's actions as Procopius does for Belisarius'. It seems rather unlikely that the Vandal king had no idea at all of the approaching Roman fleet. Carthage was the western Mediterranean's pre-eminent port, and with all the shipping going back and forth, word of Belisarius' arrival in Sicily must have reached Gelimer's ears. Possibly he still thought they were heading for Sardinia to support Godas, and even if he had suspected an attack on Africa, he could not have recalled his fleet from Sardinia in time to do anything about it.

What Gelimer was doing in Hermione, four days' march inland, is unclear. Zacharias of Mytilene's contemporary chronicle says that he was campaigning against the Moors, but Procopius seems to imply that he was relaxing at one of his royal estates. As Gelimer had an army with him, it is not unreasonable to assume that he was indeed campaigning against the Moors on his southern frontier – especially as going so far inland would have been an odd choice for relaxation in midsummer. Why he went there with a Roman fleet so close is even more puzzling. Maybe it is true that he was unaware of their approach until the last moment. He had left a sizeable force behind at Carthage under the command of his youngest brother, Ammatas, and maybe he assumed that this would have been enough to prevent an attack on his capital.

Whatever his thinking had been before Belisarius' landing at Caput Vada, as soon as he learned the truth, Gelimer sprang into action. The first thing he did was to have luckless Hilderic killed. As Gelimer was next in line, the removal of the previous monarch made it impossible for the Romans to claim that they were supporting the 'rightful king'. Then he devised a plan to trap the Roman Army in a pincer movement. He ordered Ammatas to move with his troops from Carthage to block the Roman advance at *Decimum Miliarium*, the tenth milestone to the south east of the city. He would lead his army up from Hermione to shadow the Roman advance and attack them from the south while the enemy were engaged with Ammatas' men to the west.

'Arming the Vandals, he [Ammatas] made them ready, intending to make his attack at the opportune moment. But Gelimer was following behind, without letting it be known to us, except that on the night when we bivouacked in Grasse, scouts coming from both armies [Roman and Vandal] met each other and, after an exchange of blows, they each retired to their own camp. And in this way it became evident to us that the enemy were not far away.' (Procopius)

The Battle of Ad Decimum

The tenth milestone from Carthage was not chosen by Gelimer at random. Here a projecting headland (Cap Bon) forced the Roman fleet out to sea, where they had to break contact with the army. Furthermore the road from the south east, along which the Romans had to travel, cut through hills which would mask the Vandal movements.

Gelimer's plan was a good one. The Romans would bump up against Ammatas' army, coming from Carthage, and as they deployed Gelimer would hit them in the rear. To complete the encirclement, Gelimer detached 2,000 men, under his nephew, Gibamund, to attack the Roman left flank. All of this would be done under cover of the hills and at a point where the fleet and army would be separated.

If we assume that the total Vandal manpower was something like 30,000 men, it is probably not unreasonable to assume that around 10,000 of them would have been dispersed in garrisons, fighting the Moors, on other duties, unfit for service or otherwise not physically present at the time. Tzazon had 5,000 men with him in Sardinia, leaving around 15,000 Vandals on the field at Ad Decimum, which was the same number of men Belisarius had under his command, taking into account casualties from sickness and desertion along the way. Gibamund led 2,000 men leaving 13,000 split between Gelimer and Ammatas. Assuming Gelimer commanded the most troops, a 7,000–5,000 split is not an unreasonable guess, although it may be that Ammatas had less men that that.

Knowing that the enemy was close, but not knowing exactly where he was nor what his intentions were, Belisarius advanced cautiously, with John well out in front with 300 *bucellarii* and the 600 Huns ranging along the left (southern) flank. The main column had the bulk of the remaining cavalry in front, followed by the infantry and baggage, and probably a small mounted rearguard at the end.

In order for Gelimer's well thought-out plan to succeed, the three separate commands, operating several kilometres apart, had to hit the Romans at more or less the same time. If this happened, then the Romans would have been easily destroyed. However, there were no radio communications back then and messengers riding back and forth between the separate contingents would arrive too late with news that could be acted on in a timely fashion. Furthermore, as noted in the *Strategikon* (previously quoted), the Vandal warriors had a tendency to charge into the fray rather than wait for others to catch up. Although Belisarius did not know Gelimer's plan, he had arrayed his troops in such a way that he was ready to deal with threats from all directions.

Had Ammatas moved to the tenth milestone, formed his troops up in a good blocking position, forced the Romans to deploy, then waited for Gelimer and Gibamund's attacks, the plan probably would have succeeded. Instead, leading the head of the column with his men spread out in bands of twenty to thirty warriors strung out behind, Ammatus encountered John's 300-man advance guard. Rather than waiting for the rest of his contingent to join him, Procopius says Ammatus immediately launched a charge 'with a few men and not even the pick of the army'. John's armoured horse archers presumably showered Ammatas' men with arrows and then pulled back, shooting as they retired. Then, as the Vandals tired, they would have turned back to engage them in hand-to-hand combat. Procopius praises Ammatas' bravery, saying that he killed twelve of John's best men before being killed himself. With their leader down, the Vandals routed, sweeping up the strung-out bands who were coming up behind them. 'Thinking that their pursuers were a great multitude, they [the other Vandals] turned and joined in the flight. John and his men, killing all they came upon, advanced as far as the gates of Carthage.'

With the essential blocking position blown away by only 300 men, Gelimer's plan was already beginning to unravel. But worse was to come. At this point Gibamund's 2,000 warriors had reached the salt flats of Pedion Halon, about 8km to the south west in an area, according to Procopius, 'destitute of human habitation or trees or anything else.' In this desolate place they encountered Belisarius' Huns. It was perfect terrain for the fast-moving Hun horse archers, who could shoot at their enemy and keep out of harm's way without ever giving the Vandals the opportunity to come into close contact. Procopius says that the Vandals never had any experience of battle with the Huns and did not know what to do. They broke ranks in an attempt to catch the highly mobile Huns, who continually shot at them and then turned back to pick off the stragglers. As a result, the whole of Gibamund's contingent was destroyed by less than half their number.

From Belisarius' point of view these were mere skirmishes, involving less than 1,000 of his men, while nearly half of Gelimer's army had been routed or destroyed and the plan to trap the Romans between three contingents had already failed. Neither of the principals knew this at the time, as these engagements occurred at some distance from the main columns.

Unaware of the success of his advance and flank guards, Belisarius left his infantry to establish a camp with the baggage (and his wife Antonia who, amazingly, had accompanied him), 35 stades (8km) from Decimum. Then he advanced with all the remaining cavalry. Procopius records: 'For it did not seem to him advantageous for the present to risk an engagement with the whole army, but it seemed wise to skirmish first with the horsemen and make trial of the enemy's strength and later to fight a decisive battle with the whole army.'

Belisarius' main body was led by the *foederati*, followed up by the remaining 800 *bucellarii* under Uliaris, and then the rest of the regular Roman cavalry. When they reached the tenth milestone they saw the bodies of the dead from the previous skirmish, but did not know what had happened nor what to do. Then, suddenly, a cloud of dust announced the arrival of a large force of Vandal cavalry coming up from the south. This was the advance guard of Gelimer's main column which 'was following a road between the one Belisarius was traveling and the one by which the Massagetae [Huns] who encountered Gibamund had come. Since the land was hilly on both sides it did not allow him [Gelimer] to see either the disaster of Gibamund nor Belisarius' stockade, nor even the road along which Belisarius' men were advancing.'

The lead Vandals attacked the Roman column, vieing with them for possession of the highest of the hills that dominated the area. Arriving first, the Vandals took the high ground and routed the Romans cavalry who had contested it with them. When the routing Romans galloped back to meet up with the *bucellarii*, despite their elite status, the *bucellarii* also fled rather than hold the line. Victory now seemed in Gelimer's grasp. All he had to do was follow up the breakthrough with all his forces in typical Germanic fashion. Instead, something very strange happened.

'From then on I am unable to say what happened to Gelimer. Having victory in his hands, he willingly gave it over to the enemy,' Procopius recounts. 'If he had made the pursuit immediately, I do not think that even Belisarius would have withstood him, but our cause would have been utterly and completely lost, so numerous appeared the force of the Vandals and so great the fear they inspired in the Romans. Or if on the other hand they had even ridden straight for Carthage, he [Gelimer] would easily have killed all of John's men, who, heedless of everything else, were wandering about the plain one by one or by twos and stripping the dead.' (Procopius)

The story is so strange as to seem unbelievable. If it wasn't for the fact that Procopius also expresses his incredulity, we should probably dismiss it as propaganda aimed at ruining the reputation of an enemy. What happened was that, on discovering the body of his younger brother Ammatas on the field at Decimum, Gelimer halted. He insisted on personally taking care of the burial arrangements rather than continuing the attack. This gave Belisarius time to rally his troops, form them back up, admonish them for their cowardice and launch a counterattack. He caught Gelimer's men in disarray, killed many of them and routed the rest.

The encounter at the tenth milestone was probably more a series of skirmishes over a wide area rather than a set piece battle. It was fought exclusively between small bands of mounted warriors, where advantage could be seized, lost and then won back again. It showed that the Vandals had no answer to Roman and Hun horse archery and that a very small number of determined Vandal warriors could rout even the best Roman troops by fear alone. It also showed the limitations of command and control in an ancient battle, particularly when the troops involved would decide to do as they pleased rather than stick to a plan. The armies had been probably about equal in numbers, but Belisarius' dispositions and his more flexible troops won the day, while Gelimer's sound plan was too complicated for the command and control limitations of his day.

The Romans Take Carthage

Rather than falling back on Carthage, the Vandals fled 200km west to the plains of Bulla in Numidia. One would have thought that Gelimer would have chosen to retire to Carthage and make a second stand there. However, John was already at the outskirts and according to Procopius the walls of the city had been so neglected that in many places they had fallen down, leaving gaps through which attackers could easily pass. He gives this as the reason that Gelimer did not make any attempt to hold the city. Presumably Gelimer felt that Carthage was not defensible, with a largely hostile Roman population and crumbling walls. By falling back onto the countryside he could regroup and then strike again.

The following evening, the victorious Romans marched into Carthage. The citizens threw open the gates and lit torches. 'The city was brilliant with the illumination that whole night, and those of the Vandals who had been left behind were sitting as supplicants in the sanctuaries,' writes Procopius.

Belisarius took great care to ensure that his troops behaved well and did not plunder the city. This was no mean feat as 'Roman soldiers were not accustomed to enter a subject city without confusion, even if they only numbered five hundred and especially if they made the entry unexpectedly,' Procopius recounts.

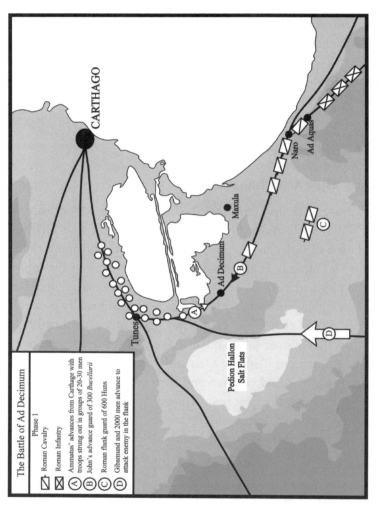

The Battle of Ad Decimum. Opening Moves. Gelimer intended to pin the advancing Roman Army with a blocking force from Carthage led by Ammatas, while Gimbamund would attack the flank with 2,000 warriors. He would follow up behind with the main body of Vandals to hit the Romans in the rear. Belisarius deployed an advance guard of 300 *bucellarii* and a flank guard of 600 Huns. His main body was led by the cavalry, with infantry following up behind.

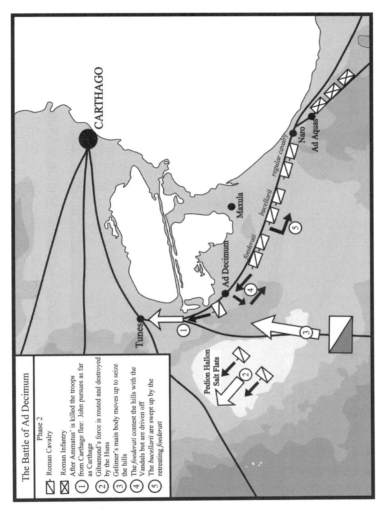

The Battle of Ad Decimum. Initial Contact. Once the advance forces came into contact all plans fell apart. Ammatas, was killed when he charged with only a few troops, while the Huns destroyed Gibamund's contingent. When Gelimer arrived on the scene he seized the high ground, driving off the Roman *foederati*, who then swept up the *bucellarii* in their retreat.

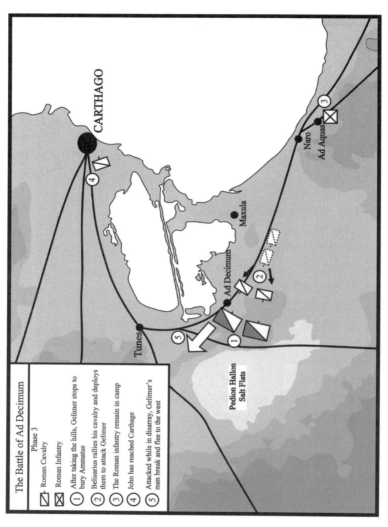

Battle of Ad Decimum. Roman Victory. On discovering the body of his brother, Ammatas, Gelimer snatched defeat from the jaws of victory by stopping to honour his brother's remains rather than continuing his pursuit of the fleeing Romans. Belisarius rallied his troops and swept the disordered Vandals from the field.

'Yet all the soldiers under the command of the general [Belisarius] showed themselves so orderly that there was not a single act of insolence nor a threat, and indeed nothing happened to hinder the business of the city.... On the contrary, the clerks drew up lists of the men and conducted the soldiers to their lodgings as usual [billeted amongst the population] and the soldiers themselves getting their lunch by purchase from the market, rested as each one wished.'

Gelimer regrouped in Numidia, where he tried to win over some of the Moors and encourage dissension amongst the population against Roman rule. He had some minor success, but it was too little and too late. In return for a bounty, some of the local peasants killed camp followers from the Roman Army and brought the heads to Gelimer for a reward, claiming that they had killed soldiers. Had the Vandals made efforts to integrate the Roman Africans and accommodate the Moors in the previous decades, then maybe they would have received greater support from them when the chips were down. A few Moors did join Gelimer, but most sent envoys to Belisarius to renew their old allegiance to the Roman Empire. In return for gifts, many Moors promised to fight for Belisarius; some even gave their children as hostages. However, until the final outcome of the war became clearer the majority stayed out of the fighting without actively supporting either side.

The Vandal King made overtures to the Visigoths in Spain seeking an alliance. However, alliances are best forged from a position of strength, and after years of enmity there was little the Vandals could now give to tempt the Visigoths to offer aid. Gelimer's envoys had set out before the Battle of Ad Decimum, but by the time they reached Spain they had been overtaken by a fast boat which carried the news of the Vandal defeat. There was no chance that the Visigoths were going to support their old enemy when their fortunes now seemed in decline.

Gelimer was later reinforced by Tzazon, who returned from Sardinia after defeating Godas. Interestingly, Procopius says that, after landing back in Africa, Tzazon and his men proceeded on foot to join the main Vandal army. Probably this was because Tzazon had not taken any horses on the sea voyage to attack Sardinia. If so, this means that the Vandals had not entirely forgotten how to fight on foot, even if their preference was clearly to mount up. In all probability, Tzazon's 5,000 men would have been able to resupply themselves with horses once back in Africa.

Over the autumn of 533, while Belisarius was improving the fortifications at Carthage and consolidating his position, Gelimer did his best to deny his enemy the surrounding countryside. Skirmishes were fought between small groups of Vandals and Romans, with the local peasants benefiting by informing on both sides. In one incident, excitingly and colourfully recounted by Procopius, Diogenes – Belisarius's aide – led twenty-two *bucellarii* on a reconnaissance patrol. Informed by farmers of their presence, Gelimer sent 300 Vandal horsemen against them with orders to capture the Romans alive.

Before dawn, the Vandals surrounded a house where Diogenes and his men were sleeping upstairs, unaware that there were any enemy nearby. 'It would have been possible for them [the Vandals] with no trouble, by carrying torches or even without these, to catch their enemies in their beds not only without weapons, but absolutely naked besides.' However, the Vandals decided to wait until first light rather than attack in the dark, when things might go awry in the confusion of a night attack.

Fortunately for the Romans, one soldier woke and heard noises outside as the Vandals moved about with their weapons and talked quietly amongst themselves. He silently woke his comrades and, without alerting the Vandals, Diogenes and his men were able to dress and go down below where their horses were stabled.

'There they put the bridles on their horses and leaped upon them unperceived by anyone. And after standing for a time by the court-yard entrance, they suddenly opened the door there, and straightway all came out. And then the Vandals immediately closed with them, but they accomplished nothing. For the Romans rode hard, covering themselves with their shields and warding off their assailants with their spears. And in this way Diogenes escaped the enemy, losing two of his followers, but saving the rest. He himself, however, received three blows in this encounter on the neck and the face, from which indeed he came within danger of dying. As a result of one blow on the left hand, he was thereafter unable to move his little finger.' (Procopius)

The Battle of Tricamarum

Even if the strategic situation favoured a long war of attrition, Gelimer's kingship would not survive it. A Germanic king's position rested on his ability to win wars and reward his followers. Gelimer had the support of the Vandal nobles on just such a promise. Hilderic had been seen to be weak, while Gelimer had promise as an able warrior. Now having lost a battle and Carthage, Gelimer had to lead his men to a decisive victory over the Romans or he would likely be overthrown, just as he had overthrown his uncle. Therefore, Gelimer marshalled his forces and marched on Carthage in December 533. He cut the aqueduct, blocked the roads and made overtures to the Huns in Belisarius' army, trying to tempt them to switch sides, but without success.

Belisarius could no more afford a war of attrition than Gelimer. He had won the first battle and captured the capital but his position was not sustainable in the long run while Gelimer still had control of much of the countryside. Although he had reinforced the defences of Carthage, Belisarius preferred open battle to being cooped up under siege. He sent out most of his cavalry in skirmish order to seek out the Vandal camp, following up behind with the infantry, 500 regular cavalry and his inner guard. They found Gelimer at a place called Tricamarum, about 28kms west of Carthage, and set up a camp on the other side of a small stream which separated the two armies.

Barbarian kings in this period typically travelled with their treasure and important members of their family. It was too dangerous to leave them behind where they could be captured without the army to protect them. Gelimer was no different. He had with him not only women and children, but also the bulk of the royal treasury. On Belisarius' approach, Gelimer had the non-combatants seek refuge inside a stockade while both he and Tzazon gave speeches to encourage their men. The gist of these pre-battle speeches was to remind the Vandals that they were fighting not only to regain their territory, but also for the lives of their families and to remain as free men. If Procopius is to be believed, given that he was not actually present with the Vandal army, Tzazon took his Sardinian veterans off to one side and reminded them of their victory over Godas and that they would need to bolster the resolve of the other Vandals who had lost at Ad Decimum.

Then Gelimer led his army out and deployed for battle. Apparently, and surprisingly, he took the Romans off-guard while they were preparing a midday meal on the opposite side of the stream that separated the two armies. At this point only the Roman cavalry, who had been sent on ahead, were immediately opposite the Vandals, with Belisarius still on the way. The Romans hastily formed up, with the left wing consisting of six cavalry units, probably each around 500 men strong. Procopius names the commanders. They were Martinus, Valerian, John, Cyprianus, Althias and Marcellus. The right was held by three units under Pappas, Barbatus and Aigan the Hun; however, the majority of the Huns were held back in reserve as their loyalty was doubtful. While the Romans were forming up, Belisarius arrived with his cavalry and deployed in the centre, leaving the infantry behind to catch up when they could. This gave the Romans a strength of about 5,000 cavalry, with no infantry.

The Vandal army must have been much larger. Tzazon's contingent alone was close to 5,000 men. The Sardinian veterans formed the centre, with the survivors of Ad Decimum deployed on each flank. A contingent of allied Moors, whose allegiance was probably even more doubtful than that of Belisarius' Huns, was kept in reserve behind the centre. Gelimer rode up and down the Vandal line urging them on to do great deeds and ordering them to fight hand-to-hand with swords only. Strangely, despite having caught the Romans off-guard he did not immediately lead them in a charge. Had he done so, particularly before Belisarius' arrival, he may have well swept the Romans from the field. Perhaps he had been scarred by the experience of Ad Decimum, where the Romans melted away from the initial charges and then came back into the attack when the Vandals were in disorder. So Gelimer waited for the Romans to make the first move.

For a long time nothing happened. The two armies faced each other across the stream, which was not a major obstacle. It did not even merit a name and was easily fordable all along its length. Belisarius decided to probe the Vandal centre and try to entice them into an uncontrolled advance, so he could then cut them down once their ranks fell into disorder. This had worked against Ammatas previously and the armoured Roman horse archers excelled at such tactics.

Belisarius sent John the Armenian with a small number of picked men, probably only a few hundred, to cross the stream and loose their arrows against Tzazon's men. So far still undefeated, Tzazon's contingent was the heart of the Vandal army and Belisarius probably counted on low morale amongst the survivors of Ad Decimum on the wings. They would be less inclined to charge forward and could be held by the Roman flanking troops, while Tzazon's men might be enticed forward.

The first Roman attack in the centre did indeed draw Tzazon forward, but as John's horse archers fell back the Vandals drew up when they came to the stream and did not follow across in pursuit. Belisarius sent John forward again with more troops, including some of the *bucellarii*. The result was much the same. The Romans rode forward, discharged volleys of arrows and then retired, but still Tzazon's men held their ranks. With the wings facing each other across the stream and Gelimer apparently making no attempt to seize the initiative, Belisarius sent even more men into the centre, including almost all of his *bucellarii*.

This time it came to hand-to-hand combat. Carrying Belisarius' standard, John charged into the Vandal ranks, probably after another volley of arrows. In close combat the Vandals would normally have had the edge over their Roman opponents, but they had been weakened by successive feints and taken casualties in both men and horses from archery, to which they had no response. In the fierce close combat, Tzazon was fighting in the front rank of the Vandals and as the battle hung in the balance he fell. With their leader killed, the Vandals in the centre began to waver and at that moment Belisarius sent his whole army forward. Procopius recounts: 'Crossing the river, they [the Romans] advanced upon the enemy and the rout, beginning in the centre, became complete. For each of the Roman divisions turned to flight those before them with no trouble.'

The Aftermath of Battle

The retreating Vandals made for the safety of their stockaded camp while the Roman, Hun and Herul cavalry stripped the dead of their armour and valuable possessions. At this stage the Romans had suffered only fifty casualties to 800 Vandal dead. The bulk of the Vandal army was, therefore, still relatively intact. They had probably only suffered a few casualties from Roman archery, with more coming from the hand-to-hand combat and the majority at the hands of their pursuers once they broke. Tzazon's death had been the turning point which shattered their morale. Warfare in this period was very personal, with the kings and princes the personification of the army. While they fought in the front rank the men fought hard alongside them, but when the leader fell a battle was often as good as lost.

Inside their fortified camp the surviving Vandals still outnumbered Belisarius' cavalry, and if they had held their nerve they could possibly have made a stand. However, when the 10,000 Roman infantry came onto the field in the late afternoon, Gelimer gave up the battle as lost and fled with some of his family. Leaderless, the Vandal army disintegrated, leaving the camp undefended.

'And the Romans, coming up, captured the camp, money and all, with not a man in it; and they pursued the fugitives throughout the whole night, killing all the men upon whom they happened, and making slaves of the women and children. And they found in this camp a quantity of wealth such as has never before been found, at least in one place. For the Vandals had plundered the Roman domain for a long time and had transferred great amounts of money to Libya, and since their land was an especially good one, nourishing abundantly with the most useful crops, it came about that the revenue collected from the commodities produced there was not paid out to any other country in the purchase of a food supply, but those who possessed the land always kept for themselves the income from it for the ninety-five years during which the Vandals ruled Libya. And from this it resulted that their wealth, amounting to an extraordinary sum, returned once more on that day into the hands of the Romans.' (Procopius)

All discipline in the Roman Army fell apart as the soldiers helped themselves to this huge wealth, not to mention the women whom Procopius describes as 'young and extremely comely'. Had Gelimer been able to gather the fugitives and launch a counterattack he would have certainly destroyed the Romans. Belisarius was very worried that this might happen but it was not until the following morning that he was able to gather together 200 *bucellarii* and send them, under John's command, to chase after Gelimer, while he did his best to restore order and then follow up behind John with a larger force.

John the Armenian pursued Gelimer for five days before he came close enough to make an attempt to capture him. Fortunately for Gelimer, John was mortally wounded by an arrow shot by Uliaris, the same man who had commanded the 800 *bucellarii* at Ad Decimum. This was not an assassination attempt. Apparently Uliaris was drunk and took a pot shot at a bird. The arrow missed, hitting John in the neck. Uliaris fled to seek sanctuary in a nearby village and John's leaderless soldiers gave up the pursuit.

Gelimer took refuge in a fortress on Mount Papua, somewhere on the extreme frontiers of Numidia, south west of Hippo Regius. The place was too strong for Belisarius to assault so he left Pharas, the Herul, with his 400 countrymen and a small number of Romans to blockade Gelimer's mountain refuge while he went back to Hippo Regius. There he took oaths from the Vandals in the city and sent them to Carthage under guard. He also got his hands on the remainder of Gelimer's royal treasure.

Strengths and Weaknesses

It is difficult to understand why the Vandal wings at Tricamarum made no move against the Romans, why Gelimer apparently did nothing to support his brother in the centre and how, therefore, 5,000 Roman cavalry were able to defeat an army which probably outnumbered them by about 3:1. Even Procopius was apparently at a loss to explain it:

'I am not able to say, wherein the fourth descendant of Geiseric and his kingdom at the height of its wealth and military strength, were so completely undone in so short a time by 5,000 men.... For such was the number of horsemen who followed Belisarius and carried the whole war against the Vandals.'

Gelimer was a respected leader, even if he lacked the mettle of the illustrious Geiseric. Indeed, he had been able to usurp the kingdom from Hilderic because he was judged to be one of the finest warriors of his generation. Neither was he stupid. His plan to entrap the Roman Army at Ad Decimum was well thought out, if too ambitious for his men to carry out given their temperament. Twice, however, Gelimer managed to snatch defeat from he jaws of victory. At Ad Decimum he stopped to bury his brother when he should have pressed home the attack. At Tricamarum he failed to attack the Romans when he had them at a disadvantage. He completely surrendered the initiative and allowed Tzazon to do all the fighting without apparently doing anything to support him.

The only possible explanation is that Gelimer had learned the lesson of Ad Decimum too well. There, his men were defeated when they charged impetuously and were cut down by the Romans when they fell into disorder. Clearly he ordered his men to hold the line and not go charging off on their own. The fact that Tzazon chased off the first few Roman attacks and then did not go beyond the stream in pursuit is testament to their control. The orders were probably something like: 'Fight well men but do not pursue the Romans beyond the stream.' The Vandal command and control limitations were such that it was apparently impossible for Gelimer to change orders mid-battle to exploit opportunities or to deal with the unexpected. This was what Belisarius excelled at. Man for man, the Vandals were probably more than a match for their Roman opponents, but they lacked tactical finesse and did not have a balanced army.

It is also worth noting the limitations of the sixth century Roman Army. At Ad Decimum, John did well in the initial encounter with Ammatas but then went riding off towards Carthage without bothering to send a messenger back to Belisarius to tell him what happened. Then, when Gelimer's force took the high ground, 800 of Belisarius' best men ran off without engaging. To be fair, they may have been ordered not to engage decisively and to fall back on the main body if large numbers of Vandals arrived. However, Procopius' rather despairing account indicates that they should have done more. It is also hard to imagine Julius Caesar's troops casually preparing a midday meal and then being caught off-guard when the enemy formed up for battle.

Once Belisarius arrived on the field of battle he took firm control and stayed out of the fighting so that he could oversee the feeding in of successive contingents to weaken the Vandal centre while keeping the enemy wings at bay. His troops then did what they were good at: riding up to the enemy, loosing their arrows and then falling back in an attempt to draw them out. When this did not succeed, they also showed that they were more than capable of engaging the best Vandal warriors in close combat and beating them at it. Had the hand-to-hand fighting taken place when Tzazon's men were still fresh, no doubt the Vandals would have had the best of it. Belisarius, however, kept the Vandal centre constantly engaged, feeding in successive waves of fresh troops, while the Vandals had no relief. In many ways this was the classic Roman way of fighting, harking back to the days of the Republic when lines of legionaries relieved each other to keep up a constant pressure on the enemy line with fresh troops. Belisarius' men may have been mounted archers but even if the soldiers were entirely different from the legionaries of old and lacked much of their discipline, the science of war had not completely died out amongst their descendants.

Mopping Up

Belisarius set about reclaiming the outlying Vandal possessions. He sent Cyril with a large force to Sardinia, along with Tzazon's head as proof of the Roman victory to cow the Vandal garrison into surrender. Another John, not the Armenian, who had died from his arrow wound, went west to take over the Mauretanias, even occupying Septem on the Straits of Gibraltar. Minorca, Majorca and the Balearic Isles were taken over by Apollinarius, a Roman from Italy who had been in Hilderic's service and was imprisoned by Gelimer after his coup. Other troops went east to support Pudentius and Tattimuth in Tripolitania.

Roman troops also went to Sicily to take over Lilybaeum, which had been given to the Vandals by the Ostrogoths as part of Amalafrida's dowry. The Goths, however, would have none of it. Their troops garrisoned the town and they had no intention of handing it over to the Romans. After a flurry of diplomatic exchanges, Belisarius backed down and referred the matter to Constantinople for Justinian's decision. The outcome of this decision, and the war that followed between the Romans and Ostrogoths, belongs to the next book in this series.

Meanwhile, Gelimer was spending a lonely, hungry winter on Mount Papua. At some point Pharas' Heruls, weary of the tedious blockade, made an attempt to take it by force. The Vandals easily drove them back, inflicting 110 casualties. However, conditions for Gelimer and his family became increasingly unbearable. According to Procopius, when Gelimer saw two children fighting over a scrap of bread he agreed to terms. These were, as Procopius recounts:

'It is the wish of the Emperor Justinian to have you enrolled in the senate, thus sharing in the highest honour and being a patrician, as we term that rank, and to present you with lands both spacious and good and with great sums of money, and that Belisarius is willing to make himself responsible for you having all these things, and to give you pledges.'

And so in early spring 534 Gelimer surrendered, bringing to an end the kingdom founded by Geiseric ninety-five years earlier. We are told that when Gelimer came before Belisarius he laughed inappropriately, leaving observers to conclude that he had lost his mind.

On 13 April 534, the Emperor Justinian issued orders for the administration of the once again Roman province of Africa. Archelaus was appointed praetorian prefect and Belisarius was given the choice of either returning to Constantinople or remaining in Africa. Belisarius chose to return, bringing with him Gelimer and several thousand Vandal prisoners. Procopius says that already people envious of Belisarius' success were slandering him to the Emperor and so, in the brittle political climate of the age, it made sense for Belisarius to go home.

When he arrived at Constantinople, Belisarius was granted a triumph. This was the first time since Augustus that a Roman general, who was not also Emperor, had been granted such an honour. On foot, rather than in the traditional chariot, Belisarius made his way from his house to the Hippodrome, where he displayed the spoils of war in front of the Imperial box. Procopius describes the booty:

'Thrones of gold and carriages in which it is customary for a king's consort to ride, and much jewellery made of precious stones, and golden drinking cups, and all the other things which are useful for the royal table. And there was also silver weighing many thousands of talents and all the royal treasure amounting to an exceedingly great sum... and among these were the treasures of the Jews, which Titus, the son of Vespasian, together with certain others, had brought to Rome after the capture of Jerusalem [and in turn looted by Geiseric in 455].... And there were slaves in the triumph, among whom was Gelimer himself, wearing some sort of a purple garment upon his shoulders, and all his family, and as many of the Vandals who were very tall and fair of body.... The Emperor Justinian and the Empress Theodora presented the children of Hilderic and his offspring and all those of the family of the Emperor Valentinian with sufficient sums of money.'

Gelimer was given a sumptuous estate in Galatia in which to live out his exile with his family. He was not, however, made a patrician as per the terms of his surrender since he refused to give up his Arian faith, which Justinian had set as a precondition. The other male Vandal prisoners met a less gruesome fate than that which befell prisoners of war in Roman triumphs of an earlier age. The new Christian Empire had long ago banned bloodthirsty spectacles in the arenas so, rather than fighting each other for the amusement of the crowd, the Vandals formed the basis of five new units sent off to defend the Empire's eastern frontier against Persia.

Chapter 8

Moors and Mutineers

The Taxman Cometh

On 1 January 535, Belisarius was made Consul. The Vandal Kingdom had been destroyed, Roman rule had returned to Africa and the local populace were now free to practice their Catholic faith without fear of persecution. From the Roman point of view, all should have been well and in other circumstances our story would end here. But all was not well.

By and large the Moors had waited out the struggle between Belisarius and Gelimer without committing themselves. A number had been on the battlefield at Tricamarum in support of the Vandals, but they took no active part in the fighting. Later, some Moors gave sanctuary to Gelimer on Mount Papua, even helping him fight off the assault by Pharas' Heruls. The majority, however, pledged their allegiance to Belisarius as soon as it was clear that he was in the ascendancy.

As soon as they heard that Belisarius was leaving, however, the Moors of Byzacena and Numidia took advantage of the vacuum and began to raid the outlying regions. Procopius gives a scathing verdict on their behaviour:

'For there is among the Moors neither fear of God nor respect for men. For they care not either for oaths or for hostages, even though the hostages chance to be the children or brothers of their leaders. Nor is peace maintained among the Moors by any other means than by fear of the enemies opposing them.'

We have already seen how oaths of allegiance in this period of history were very personal, given to an individual and not to a nebulous concept such as a state or nation. Just as Geiseric did not feel bound by a treaty he had signed with Valentinian III once the Emperor had been murdered, neither did the Moors feel honour bound to uphold agreements made with Belisarius once the general took ship for Constantinople. The Romans assumed treaties were made with the Empire while the barbarian tribes gave oaths to individuals.

The defence of Roman Africa was entrusted to Solomon. Although Belisarius took some of his closest followers with him to Constantinople, he decided it best to leave the bulk of the Roman Army, including most of his *bucellarii*, behind with Solomon so that he had sufficient forces to deal with the Moors. The Emperor also sent further reinforcements under Theodorus, the Cappadocian, and Ildiger. Unhelpfully, Justinian also sent two tax officials, Tryphon and Eustratius, to assess the tax owing to the Empire by the native Roman Africans. This would have taken more than a little of the gloss off the Roman victory, as Procopius says that the taxmen were 'neither moderate nor endurable'.

While Justinian's tax inspectors were busily assessing the wealth that could be sucked out of North Africa, the Moors destroyed the outlying Roman garrisons in Byzacena and Numidia. Two detachments of Roman cavalry, commanded by Aigan the Hun and Rufinus the Thracian, came across a band of Moors in Byzacena who were plundering the farms and carrying off captives. They ambushed the raiders in a narrow pass and defeated them. However, a much larger Moorish army was close by. It was led by four chieftains, named by Procopius as Coutzinas, Esdilasas, Iourphouthes and Medisinissas. They attacked the small Roman force, trapping them in the pass. As long as the Romans and Huns could use their bows they were able to keep the Moors at bay, but when they ran out of arrows the Moors closed in for the kill and destroyed them. Aigan had commanded one of the contingents on the right wing at Tricamarum and Rufinus was Belisarius' standard bearer. Aigan was killed in the fighting while Rufinus was captured and then beheaded by Medisinissas, who took the head back to show his wives. Procopius says that 'it was a remarkable sight on account of the extraordinary size of the head and the abundance of hair.'

Camels, Mountains and Duels

The loss of two respected officers from Belisarius' *bucellarii* shocked the Romans. Solomon immediately marched against the Moors with his army, finding them encamped at a place called Mammes on the borders of Mauretania. As the Roman Army approached, the Moors formed a circle of camels on a plain at the foothills of the mountains, just as Cabon had done when he took on the Vandals. Women, children and baggage took refuge in the middle of the circle while most of the fighting men, on foot and armed with light javelins, arrayed themselves around the perimeter. A body of mounted men remained outside the camel circle, hidden in the foothills, ready to sweep down at the right moment. Solomon concentrated his whole army against the part of the circle furthest from the mountains, possibly aware of the Moorish cavalry who were stationed there.

After the traditional pre-battle speeches, in which each commander urged his men to fight bravely and reminded them of previous victories, Solomon launched his attack. The Romans had to deal with the same problem that had plagued Thrasamund's Vandals a few years earlier.

'For their horses were offended by the noise made by the camels and by the sight of them, and reared up and threw off their riders and the most of them fled in complete disorder. And in the meantime the Moors were making sallies and hurling all the small spears which they had in their hands, thus causing the Roman Army to be filled with tumult, and they were hitting them with their missiles while they were unable either to defend themselves or to remain in position.' (Procopius)

The Roman soldiers where, however, more flexible than the Vandals. Seeing that the horses would not close with the camels, Solomon ordered his men to dismount. Leading 500 of them, their shields covering them to ward off the Moorish javelins, Solomon attacked the camel circle and broke through. Once the gap was opened, the rest of the Roman Army poured through and the Moors fled, leaving their women and children to their fate.

Solomon fought a second battle against another army of Moors who, after ravaging Byzacena, had holed up in a mountain refuge. Their stronghold was a place called Mount Bourgaon by Procopius, which was presumably somewhere on the south western borders of modern Tunisia. Solomon deployed for battle, hoping that the Moors would come down from the mountain to attack him, but they did not oblige.

The eastern slope of the mountain was very steep, while the western side had a gentle slope. Naturally the Moors faced the Romans on the western slope, trusting that no attack could come from the east. Solomon took advantage of this, sending Theodorus, who led an elite guards unit of 1,000 men known as *Excubitores,* to climb the eastern slope in late afternoon. They reached the summit in the middle of the night, unobserved by the Moors. At dawn, Solomon attacked from the west, while Theodorus descended from the summit in the east, pinning the Moors between them.

Defeating the Moors must have seemed to Solomon like trying to hold back the tide. He had only one army and not a large one, while his enemies were an innumerable number of bands that ranged all along the frontiers. No sooner had one been put down than another popped up somewhere else. While Solomon was clearing out Byzacena, another Moorish chieftain, by the name of Iaudas, was ravaging Numidia, joined by the survivors of Solomon's victories at Mammes and Mount Bourgaon.

Procopius describes a fascinating incident when a Roman officer by the name of Althias led seventy Huns to capture a spring near where Iaudas' men were raiding. It was midsummer. The Moors had been in the saddle all day and there were no other water sources nearby. Although the Moors greatly outnumbered Althias' Huns, when they reached the spring to find it in enemy hands they were worn out, thirsty and their horses were spent. Althias refused a deal to take a share of the Moors' booty in exchange for access to the well. Instead he challenged Iaudas to single combat. Procopius relates:

'It was agreed that if it so fell out that Althias was overcame, the Moors should drink. And the whole Moorish army was rejoiced, being in good hope, since Althias was lean and not tall of body, while Iaudas was the finest and most warlike of all the Moors. Now both of them were, as it happened, mounted. And Iaudas hurled his spear first, but as it was coming toward him Althias succeeded with amazing skill in catching it with his right hand, thus filling Iaudas and the enemy with consternation. And with his left hand he drew his bow instantly, for he was ambidextrous, and hit and killed the horse of Iaudas. And as he fell, the Moors brought another horse for their commander, upon which Iaudas leaped and straightway fled; and the Moorish army followed him in complete disorder. And Althias, by thus taking from them the captives and the whole of the booty, won a great name in consequence of this deed throughout all Libya.'

This incident gives us some insight into the nature of sixth century warfare, with its heroic ethos in which the prowess and deeds of the leaders were of utmost importance. It also shows us how much the ideal Roman soldier had changed from the steady legionary of old to a mounted warrior capable of using different weapons with amazing dexterity. Thus the deeds of a few skilled notable men, whether Vandal, Moor or Roman, could decide the outcome and bring victory or defeat to their followers.

The Moors were not a single nation. When Solomon marched against Iaudas with his full army, two other Moorish chieftains, Massonas and Ortaias, joined him as Iaudas had expanded his power at their expense. With his new Moorish allies Solomon marched to confront Iaudas, who, typically, had a mountain stronghold on Mount Aurasium. Solomon's attempt to take the mountain failed because his enemies fell back rather than offering battle. As the Roman Army's supplies began to dwindle, Solomon had to give up the fight. Leaving a force to bottle up the Moors in the Aurès Mountains, he returned to Carthage with the rest of his army with the intention of renewing the offensive in the spring of 536.

Mutiny

Solomon was clearly a very capable commander. He had shown great initiative and flexibility in dealing with the Moors, adapting his tactics to suit the situation. Without other problems to deal with, he probably would have eventually been successful. So far he had been dealt a pretty difficult hand, but he played the cards well and stayed in the game. By Easter 536, his hand was so bad that he could no longer win on skill alone.

The first problem was that many of the Roman soldiers in Africa had married Vandal widows or their daughters, assuming that they would take over the Vandal estates that had previously belonged to their husbands or fathers. With Justinian's tax collectors at large, it was the Imperial treasury, not the veteran soldiers, who would gain the fruits of victory. A soldier married to a Vandal woman who previously owned the land, now became a tenant farmer and had to pay tax to the Imperial treasury. He would have seen the ships leaving for Constantinople, ladened with treasure he had fought to win. Adding insult to injury, neither he nor his comrades had been paid in months. Justinian went to the trouble of sending tax collectors but not to send any money to pay the soldiers who had fought for him.

Another old problem also raised its ugly head. Many of the Roman soldiers were of Germanic origin, and as such were Arians. This was certainly true of the Heruls in the army, but also many of the regular cavalry would have been recruited from other Arian German tribes. One of Justinian's motivations for his war against the Vandals had been to restore orthodox Nicene Christianity, and he did this with a vengeance. In an attempt to stamp out the Arian faith, the Emperor decreed that no one would be allowed to be baptized as an Arian. By 536, many of the Roman soldiers who had taken Vandal wives now had children ready for baptism, and with Easter approaching they would not be allowed unless they renounced their faith.

Mutiny was brewing, bolstered by 400 Vandals who had been shipped earlier to Constantinople along with the other prisoners of war. En route they had managed to take over the ships carrying them and made them turn back to Africa.

'They [the Vandals] came to land in Libya at a desert place, where they abandoned the ships, and, after equipping themselves, went up to Mount Aurasium and Mauretania. Elated by their accession, the soldiers who were planning the mutiny formed a still closer conspiracy among themselves. And there was much talk about this in the camp and oaths were already being taken. And when the rest were about to celebrate the Easter festival, the Arians, being vexed by their exclusion from the sacred rites, proposed to attack them [the loyalists] vigorously.' (Procopius)

When an attempt to assassinate Solomon failed, many of the disgruntled soldiers took off to ravage the countryside around Carthage, while the loyalists and waverers gathered in the Hippodrome. Solomon sent Theodorus the Cappadocian to calm them, as he was popular with the troops. Rather than listening to him, the soldiers proclaimed him as their leader. Mutiny amongst Roman soldiers was nothing new. In previous centuries they would have lifted Theodorus on a shield and proclaimed him Emperor, in the way the British mutineers proclaimed Marcus, Gratian and Constantine earlier in our story (see Chapter 3). However, these mutineers did not have such grand plans. Indeed, it is not entirely clear what they wanted other than to get their pay, their share of the spoils and, for some of them, the right to practice their version of Christianity. When this was not forthcoming, their plan seemed to be to take over North Africa for themselves, as Odoacer's men had done with Italy in 476.

Theodorus remained loyal. He helped Solomon, Procopius and a small number of notable loyalists to escape by sea while the mutineers rampaged through Carthage and then gathered on the plains of Bulla, where Gelimer had regrouped after his defeat at Ad Decimum. There, 8,000 mutineers proclaimed Stotzas as their leader and were joined by a large number of escaped slaves. The 400 Vandals who had escaped captivity also came to them, the Vandal numbers swelling to 1,000 as they were joined by others who had so far managed to avoid capture.

The Belisarius Effect

Unfortunately for the mutineers, Belisarius was close by in spring 536. He was in Sicily, about to embark on an even grander expedition to take back Italy from the Ostrogoths. When Solomon and Procopius joined him, telling him of the dire situation in Africa, Belisarius knew he had to act. He could not afford to divert the whole army gathering for the Gothic war to go to Africa, but neither could he afford to have a hostile Africa at his back.

Trusting to his fame with his former soldiers, Belisarius took ship to Carthage with Solomon and 100 picked *bucellarii*. Theodorus was still holding the city with a small number of loyal troops, while the mutineers ranged through the surrounding countryside and were encamped around the walls. As we have already seen, the reputation of individual leaders was more important than the number of troops they commanded. Belisarius' reputation was second to none. As soon as word reached the mutineers that he had landed at Carthage they fled to Membresa (Mejaz al-Bab) on the Bagradas River, about 60km south west of Carthage. Belisarius followed hard on their heels with 2,000 loyalist troops.

Battle was joined the following day. In the traditional pre-battle speeches, Belisarius described the mutineers as 'a throng of men united by no law, but brought together by motives of injustice.' He reminded his soldiers that their good discipline and orderly array would more than make up for the enemy's larger numbers. Stotzas reminded the mutineers of the injustices done to them, saying that it was better to die fighting for freedom than to live in servitude.

Belisarius had the wind to his back, and as the two armies drew up for battle the wind became so strong as to cause the mutineers' arrows to fall short, giving extra range to those of the loyalists. Stotzas then moved out on one flank in an attempt to encircle Belisarius' smaller army. Never one to surrender the initiative, Belisarius launched an immediate attack, hitting the mutineers while their ranks were in disorder from changing formation. Most of the mutineers fled immediately without waiting to engage in close combat. As a result they suffered few casualties, and most of those were Vandals, indicating that while the mutineers turned and ran without fighting, the Vandals at least made a stand.

Job apparently done, Belisarius departed to take up the campaign against the Ostrogoths. He could not delay, as word had come from Sicily that the troops there were also in a mutinous mood. The loyalist army in Africa pursued Stotzas to Gadiaufala (Ksar-Sbehi), two days' journey from Carthage. It should have been an easy victory for them as many of the mutineers had melted away. Stotzas, however, infiltrated the enemy camp and reminded the loyal soldiers of the injustices done to them. His words are reported by Procopius, although he was not actually present:

'Fellow-soldiers, you are not acting justly in taking the field against kinsmen and those who have been reared with you, and in raising arms against men who in vexation at your misfortunes and the wrongs you have suffered have decided to make war upon the Emperor and the Romans. Or do you not remember that you have been deprived of the pay which has been owing you for a long time back, and that you have been robbed of the enemy's spoil, which the law of war has set as prizes for the dangers of battle? And that the others have claimed the right to live sumptuously all their lives upon the good things of victory, while you have followed as if their servants?'

Without the great Belisarius there to hold them together, the Imperial soldiers killed their commanders and joined in the mutiny.

The Battle of Scalae Veteres

The mutiny could easily have been prevented and, in its early stages, could probably still have been nipped in the bud if the Imperial authorities had bothered to pay the soldiers the money they were owed. In 536, Justinian did what he should have been done long before. He sent his nephew Germanus, to Africa with enough money to pay the soldiers all their wages – including back pay for the time that they had been in rebellion. On his arrival in Carthage, Germanus found that two-thirds of the army had gone over to the mutineers, but with money now forthcoming many began to trickle back.

Stotzas decided to march on Carthage and force a decisive engagement before he lost too many more troops to the Emperor's now open pay chest. However, when Germanus' increasing numbers of troops deployed to meet him, many of the mutineers broke ranks and fell back towards Numidia to protect their families and possessions. Germanus followed up, catching the mutineers at a place called Scalae Veteres.

Germanus deployed his infantry, commanded by Domicus, in the centre, along a line of wagons. He led the *bucellarii* that he had brought from Constantinople on the left wing, while the other cavalry – many of whom had recently been amongst the mutineers – were deployed in three divisions on the right. Procopius says that the mutineers formed up without order 'in the manner of the barbarians', with several thousand Moors hanging back to await the outcome before committing themselves, as usual. The surviving Vandals were also part of Stotzas' army, but Procopius does not say where they deployed nor what they did in the battle. It is possible that they were arrayed with Stotzas and the Heruls, as later they remained with the leader of the mutineers when the battle was lost.

Stotzas attempted to open the battle by leading the Heruls – and possibly the Vandals —in a charge against Germanus on the left wing, but they refused to follow him against men who seemed determined to make a good fight of it. Therefore he switched his attack to the other wing, which was held by their old comrades who would be less inclined to fight quite so enthusiastically. This initial attack succeeded and the Imperial cavalry on the right broke.

'And the mutineers took all their standards immediately, and pursued them as they fled at top speed, while some too charged upon the infantry, who had already begun to abandon their ranks. But at this juncture Germanus himself, drawing his sword and urging the whole of that part of the army to do the same, with great difficulty routed the mutineers opposed to him and advanced on the run against Stotzas.' (Procopius)

At this point the battle dissolved into groups of mounted men from both sides mingling with each other and fighting a confused melée without order.

'Neither side could be distinguished either by their own comrades or by their opponents. For all used one language and the same equipment of arms, and they differed neither in figure nor in dress nor in any other thing whatever.' (Procopius)

Germanus' horse was killed under him but he was saved at the last minute by his *bucellarii*, who formed a ring around him and gave him another horse. They pressed on with the fight and eventually gained the upper hand, managing to break into the enemy camp and begin looting it. At this point the Moors decided to join in, switching sides to chase down Stotzas' men and get their share of the loot. Stotzas made a last ditch attempt to rally the Moors back over to his side, but when this failed he fled the field with no troops other than 100 surviving Vandals.

The End of the Vandals

The mutiny was over, and so too was the hope of the few remaining free Vandals to salvage something from their once great kingdom. Over the next four years there were further mutinies amongst the Roman troops and constant battles against the Moors. In 539, Solomon finally defeated Iaudas and garrisoned Mount Aurasium, then he began re-fortifying the African cities.

'He ruled with moderation and guarded Libya securely, setting the army in order, and sending to Byzantium and to Belisarius whatever suspicious elements he found in it, and enrolling new soldiers to equal their number, and removing those of the Vandals who were left and especially all their women from the whole of Libya.' (Procopius)

However, Solomon was killed in a skirmish with the Moors of Tripolitania in 543 and his nephew, Sergius, was appointed governor of Africa in his place. Procopius is scathing in his description of him:

'This man [Sergius] became the chief cause of great ruin to the people of Libya, and all were dissatisfied with his rule – the officers because, being exceedingly stupid and young both in character and in years, he proved to be the greatest braggart of all men, and he insulted them for no just cause and disregarded them, always using the power of his wealth and the authority of his office to this end; and the soldiers disliked him because he was altogether unmanly and weak; and the Libyans, not only for these reasons, but also because he had shown himself strangely fond of the wives and the possessions of others.'

In the resulting unrest, Stotzas and the last remaining free Vandals came from the west to join up with Antalas, a Moorish chieftain who had overrun much of Byzacena and who was probably the same man who had defeated Hoamer's Vandals in the late 520s. A number of disaffected Roman soldiers also fell in behind Stotzas' standard. In 545, Justinian once again had to send reinforcements from Constantinople to deal with the chaos. He sent Areobindus with some Armenian soldiers to take over the campaign in Byzacena, leaving Sergius to deal with Numidia.

Areobindus sent a small army, commanded by yet another John, to engage Stotzas and Antalas at Sicca Venera (El Kef in modern Tunisia). He also summoned the other Roman forces to join him, but Sergius refused.

'John with a small army was compelled to engage with an innumerable host of the enemy.... As soon as the fighting was about to come to close quarters, both [John and Stotzas] rode out from their armies and came against each other. And John drew his bow, and, as Stotzas was still advancing, made a successful shot and hit him in the right groin, and Stotzas, mortally wounded, fell there, not yet dead, but destined to survive this wound only a little time.' (Procopius)

Once again we see the personal nature of sixth century warfare, with the leaders engaging in duels before the main action. In this instance Stozas, loss did result in the defeat of his army. Instead, his Vandal and Roman followers, together with Antalas' Moors, rode out to avenge him. They swept aside the smaller Roman Army, killing John in the process.

Following this disaster, Justinian recalled Sergius and sent him to Italy to support Belisarius against the Ostrogoths, leaving Africa under Areobindus' sole command. This did not last long. Gontharius, a Roman officer of Germanic origin, assassinated Areobindus in an attempt to seize Africa for himself. The remnants of Stotzas' army joined his cause. Procopius says that these numbered 1,000 men: 500 Romans and eighty Huns, with the rest being Vandals.

Gontharius broke with Antalas. His troops, including the Vandals, defeated the Moorish chieftain near Hadrumentum (Sousse), supported by other Moors who had fallen out with Antalas. After this victory Gontharius held a banquet at Carthage. Artabanes, leader of the Armenian troops sent to Africa by Justinian to support Areobindus, was one of the principal guests. He had commanded the army which defeated Antalas, but he was Areobindus' man. He had been looking for the right moment to avenge his patron's assassination. He prepared his Armenian bodyguards and, when Gontharius was 'thoroughly saturated with wine', he had them strike. Gontharius was killed, ending yet another mutiny and ending forever the hopes of the last few remaining Vandals.

'The Vandals fled to sanctuary. To these Artabanes gave pledges, and making them rise from there, sent them to Byzantium, and having thus recovered the city [Carthage] for the Emperor, he continued to guard it. And the murder of the tyrant [Gontharius] took place on the thirty-sixth day of the tyranny, in the nineteenth year of the reign of the Emperor Justinian [546].' (Procopius)

So it was, 140 years after the Vandals crossed the Rhine, they finally disappeared from history.

The Vandal Legacy

The Vandals left virtually no archeological record: no great buildings, no new art, no writers, poets or philosophers. All we really have to remember them by is their name and its modern association with wanton destruction. They came from virtual obscurity, bursting onto the Roman world from the forests of central Germany to become the pre-eminent power in the Western Mediterranean. Their's was a story of survival against all odds, a story of a people searching for an identity and a place in the civilized world. For a brief moment, under the inspired leadership of Geiseric, it looked as if they had achieved it. They held the most prosperous province of the West Roman Empire, controlled the sea and the Vandal royal family became linked in marriage to the Imperial house of Theodosius.

The descendants of Geiseric enjoyed the good life for several generations. As a small warrior aristocracy, however, they could never hope to control the vast swathes of territory they had conquered without finding some way to accommodate their more numerous Roman subjects and the many bands of Moors of the hinterland. In this regard they were far less successful than the Goths and Franks. The former made alliances with the Roman landed aristocracy and made attempts to meld the two cultures. The Franks benefited from never adopting Arian Christianity, and when they converted from paganism they followed the same orthodox beliefs as their Roman subjects.

For the Vandals, their Arian beliefs became an essential part of their identity. Their vigorous attempts to suppress the Catholic Church made integration with the Roman Africans nearly impossible. This ensured that they would never have the manpower to deal with the Moorish threats and forced the local inhabitants to look to Constantinople for their eventual salvation. Had the Vandals and Roman Africans been living in harmony, and if the Vandals had been content to be passive Arians, then maybe Justinian would not have attempted a reconquest. If he had attempted it under those circumstances, then it probably would have failed.

In their early days, the Vandals showed themselves to be incredibly resourceful and adaptable. Crossing the Rhine in midwinter was a huge gamble. The decision was probably forced on them as starvation threatened, but even though the Roman defences had been stripped to the bone the Vandals' ability to survive and a winter campaign is testament to their fortitude. Beset by a multitude of enemies – Romans, Goths, Suevi and Moors – the Vandals managed to hang on. They fought when necessary, moved on when the situation became untenable. Despite many setbacks they managed to dust themselves off, pick themselves up again and emerge stronger than before. They trekked thousands of kilometres from Germany, through France and Spain, then along the coast of North Africa. Their original landlocked homeland was as far from the sea as is possible in Europe, and yet in a single generation they became the greatest naval power in the known world.

Once they found a recipe for success they kept to it, and if adaptability had been a hallmark of the early Vandals, their successors seemed to have become stuck in their ways. Once they had settled down in Africa with all the resources they needed to equip themselves as well accoutred mounted warriors, that was how they fought— at least on land. Up against the mobile Moors, who would skirmish at a distance, evade if charged and seek refuge in mountain hideaways or behind a circle of camels, the later Vandals did not adapt their tactics to suit the situation. When the Roman general Solomon faced Moors behind a line of camels, he dismounted his cavalry to attack on foot. Thrasamund's Vandals did not do the same when they came up against Cabon's men in a similar situation, even though many of their ancestors would have often fought dismounted. Despite defeats at the hands of both the Moors and East Romans, the later Vandals never changed their fighting methods.

Other than the incredible story of their rise from obscurity to world power, probably the greatest legacy of the Vandals was to hasten the end of the West Roman Empire. Geiseric's capture of Carthage in 439 deprived Rome of her most prosperous province. It gave the Vandals control over the Western Mediterranean and the vital grain supply to Italy. With Goths, Huns, Franks, Burgundians, Saxons and Alamanni pouring over the frontiers; combined with internal strife, peasant uprisings and near perpetual war with the Persians to occupy the Eastern Empire, the West could not survive without Africa.

The little-known naval battle of Mercurium in 468 really deserves to be remembered as one of the most decisive battles of the western world. This catastrophic defeat of the huge Roman armada at the hands of the Vandals sealed Rome's fate forever. If the Romans had been victorious, then there was every possibility that a rump of the Empire could have continued in the West in much the same way as it did in the East.

It may well have been the Huns, whose westward movements sparked off the Germanic migrations of the fifth century, that brought about the beginning of the end for the West Roman Empire. It may too have been Rome's own internal weaknesses and her inability to find a way to replace an Emperor other than by a coup which made the Empire's collapse inevitable. However, it was Geiseric's Vandals who dealt the death blow in 468. Without Africa's wealth and produce to prop up Italy and fund an army, the West Roman Empire was doomed.

Do the Vandals not deserve the reputation that their name now implies? Yes, they did loot Rome for fourteen days and yes, they did carry off most of her portable wealth. But the sack of Rome in 455 was done in accordance with an agreement with the Pope and it was not a wild orgy of rape, pillage and plunder. It is true that the Vandals did persecute Catholic Christians in Africa, but their persecutions were relatively mild compared to the church's own actions against heretics in later years. Unfortunately, the Vandals did not have someone like Cassiodorus, Jordanes or Gregory of Tours, who told the stories of the Goths and Franks from their perspective. Our only glimpse into the world of the Vandals comes from their enemies, and it is little wonder that these accounts are less than favourable. Only Procopius gives us any detailed first-hand descriptions of the Vandals and these were when they were in decline. The churchmen who wrote of the Vandals in the fifth century left us only snippets and their writings were heavily biased by their animosity to the Vandal Arian faith.

For me, the story of the Vandals is one of great fortitude in the face of adversity. It is a story of the most incredible migration in history, where a whole people moved from the forests of Germany to the plains of North Africa and finally managed to find their place in the sun. It is also a story of great tragedy. The Vandals wanted acceptance in the same way as the Goths and Franks had been accepted, but they never achieved it. The Romans gave them no peace in Spain and then, once the Vandals had taken Africa, the Romans could no longer afford to do so.

Chronology

Second century BC: Ancestors of the Vandals move from Scandinavia into central Europe. Conflict between the Vandals, Lombards and Goths.

First century AD: The Vandals are living in Silesia.

Second century AD: The Asding Vandals move south into Bohemia.

166–180: The Marcomannic Wars. The Asdings expand into Dacia.

248: Asdings and Goths raid Roman Moesia.

270: The Goths defeated at the Battle of Naissus.

271: Asdings and Sarmatians defeated by the Emperor Aurelian.

274: Asding prisoners of war paraded in Aurelian's triumph.

278: Probus defeats the Silings and Burgundians on the Lech River. Vandal survivors resettled in Britain.

Early-fourth century: The Asding King Visimar defeated by the Goths at the Maros River.

341: Ulfilas begins to convert the Goths to Arian Christianity.

C.350–375: The Huns defeat the Goths and Alans, pushing them westward.

378: Gothic refugees destroy the East Roman Army at the Battle of Adrianople.

382: Goths settled in the Balkans under treaty with Theodosius.

382: Magnus Maximus proclaimed Emperor in Britain. Moving to Gaul, he establishes his capital at Trier.

388: Magnus Maximus defeated by Theodosius. The Rhine defences weakened.

392: Death of Valentinian II. Arbogast proclaims Eugenius as Western Emperor.

394: Eugenius and Arbogast defeated by Theodosius, Stilicho and Alaric at the Battle of Frigidus River.

395: Death of Theodosius. The Roman Empire divided, with the West under Honorius and the East under Arcadius. Stilicho holds supreme power. Alaric leads a rebellion of Goths in the Balkans.

c.400: Huns move further west, settling on the Hungarian plain and triggering off another wave of Germanic migrations.

401: Alaric invades Italy for the first time. Asding Vandals raid Raetia and are defeated by Stilicho.

401: Stilicho defeats Alaric.

405: Radagasius invades Italy, his army possibly including some Vandals.

406, 23 August: Radagasius defeated by Stilicho near Florence.

406: Asdings and Silings move west towards the middle Rhine frontier. Asding King Godegisel killed in battle against the Franks and the Vandals are saved from disaster by Respendial's Alans. Gunderic becomes King of the Asdings.

406: British Army revolts, proclaiming Constantine III as Emperor.

406, 31 December: Silings, Asdings, Suevi and Alans cross the Rhine.

407: Constantine III crosses into Gaul. Engagements between Constantine's forces and the barbarian invaders keep the Vandals and their allies bottled up in northern Gaul.

407-8: Rheims, Amiens, Arras, Tournai and Spires fall to the Vandals and their allies. The Burgundians take Worms and the Alamanni seize Strasbourg. Some of the Alans, under Goar, break off, make peace with the Romans and are settled near Orléans as federates. Stilicho sends Sarus against Constantine but he is defeated. Gerontius defects from Constantine and takes power in Spain.

408: Stilicho executed. Alaric again invades Italy.

409, 28 September or 13 October: The Vandals, Alans and Suevi cross into Spain.

410, 20 August: Alaric's Goths sack Rome.

411: Gerontius moves from Spain to Gaul to confront Constantine III at Arles. His army mutinies and he is killed.

411: Honorius' general Constantius defeats Constantine III.

411: The barbarians divide up Spain by lot. The Asdings settle in eastern Gallaecia; the Suevi in western Gallaecia; the Silings in Baetica; and the Alans in Lusitania and Carthaginiensis.

411: Alaric dies and is succeed by Ataulf.

414: Ataulf's Goths move into France and Spain. They capture Barcelona.

415: Ataulf murdered and succeeded by Wallia. The Goths move against the Vandals, Alans and Suevi in Spain on behalf of the Romans.

416: The Siling leader Fredibal is captured by the Goths.

418: The Silings are destroyed by the Goths and the Alans are defeated. The survivors merge with the Asdings to create the kingdom of the Vandals and Alans.

418: Wallia is murdered and Theodoric I becomes King of the Visigoths.

419: The Vandals defeat King Hermanric's Suevi. They in turn are defeated by the Romans.

422: Roman amphibious attack on the Vandals in Baetica has initial success but ends in failure.

423: Honorius dies.

425: The six-year-old Valentinian III becomes Western Emperor with his mother, Galla Placidia, the power behind the throne.

425: Vandal seaborne raids against the Balearic Isles and Mauritania.

427: Power struggle between Boniface, Felix and Aeitus.

428: Death of Gunderic. Geiseric becomes King of the Vandals and Alans.

429: The Vandals cross over to Africa.

430, May: The Vandals defeat Boniface near Hippo Regius and lay siege to the city.

430, 28 August: St. Augustine dies during the Vandal siege of Hippo Regius.

430: Aetius assassinates Felix.

432: Aspar sent from Constantinople to reinforce Boniface's defence against the Vandals. The Romans are defeated near Carthage. Boniface returns to Italy and defeats Aetius at the Battle of Rimini but is mortally wounded.

433: Rua, King of the Huns, dies and is succeeded by Attila and Bleda. Aetius is given supreme military power in the West.

435, February: The Vandal conquests are recognised by treaty, which grants them the status of Roman federates. Aspar is recalled to Constantinople. Aeitus focuses his attention on Gaul.

439, 19 October: Geiseric captures Carthage in a surprise attack.

440: The Vandals raid Sicily.

441: A large Roman fleet sets sail from Constantinople to recapture Africa but is recalled due to an invasion by Attila's Huns.

442: Treaty with Rome recognizes Geiseric as an independent allied king with control over North Africa. Huneric goes to Ravenna as a hostage. His Gothic wife, daughter of King Theodoric, is mutilated and returned to her father, creating a feud between the Vandals and Goths. Huneric is betrothed to Valentinian III's daughter Eudocia.

442: Revolt of the Vandal nobles suppressed by Geiseric.

445: A Vandal fleet raids Suevic lands on the Atlantic coast of Spain.

445: Bleda murdered. Attila becomes sole king of the Huns.

447: Attila's Huns ravage the Balkans and threaten Constantinople.

451: Attila defeated by Aeitus at the Battle of the Catalaunian Fields near Troyes in France.

452: Attila invades Italy.

453: Death of Attila.

454: The Huns are defeated at the Battle of Nedao by a coalition of Germanic tribes. Aeitus is murdered by Valentinian III.

455: Valentinian murdered. Petronius Maximus becomes Western Emperor.

455, June: The Vandals sack Rome and capture Valentinian's wife and two daughters. Huneric marries Eudocia, linking the Vandal royal family with the Imperial house of Theodosius.

455: Avitus proclaimed Western Emperor with the support of the Goths.

456: A Roman fleet defeats the Vandals off Corsica.

457: Avitus abdicates and is replaced by Majorian, with Ricimer the power behind the throne.

460: The Vandals destroy the Roman fleet gathered by Majorian at Cartagena to invade Africa.

461: Majorian executed by Ricimer, who proclaims Libius Severus as Western Emperor.

462: Valentinian's widow, Eudoxia, and youngest daughter, Placidia, are sent to Constantinople to placate the Eastern Empire.

465: Libius Severus dies and is not replaced, as Ricimer and the Eastern Empire cannot come to an agreement over his replacement.

467: Anthemius appointed Western Emperor by Constantinople with Ricimer's agreement. He brings fresh troops with him and prepares to deal with the Vandals.

468: The Battle of Mercurium. The Vandals destroy a huge Roman invasion fleet off the coast of Africa.

472, April: Anthemius deposed by Ricimer. Olybrius, Geiseric's brother-in-law, becomes West Roman Emperor.

472, 18 August: Ricimer dies.

472, November: Olybrius dies.

475: Orestes, Attila's former secretary, proclaims his son Romulus Augustulus as West Roman Emperor.

476: Odoacer leads a mutiny of the barbarian troops in the Roman Army of Italy. He overthrows Romulus and becomes King of Italy.

477, 25 January: Death of Geiseric.

477–484: Reign of Huneric. Catholics severely persecuted. Moors start to raid the frontiers of the Vandal Kingdom.

484–496: Reign of Gunthamund.

489: Ostrogoths under Theodoric invade Italy.

493: Theodoric overthrows Odoacer and becomes King of Italy.

496–523: Reign of Thrasamund. Cabon's Moors defeat the Vandals in Tripolitania.

500: Thrasamund marries Amalafrida, sister of the Ostrogothic King of Italy. Her dowry includes 5,000 Gothic troops and Lilybaeum in western Sicily.

502: War between Persia and the East Roman Empire.

507: The Visigoths in Gaul defeated by the Franks at the Battle of Vouillé.

523–530: Reign of Hilderic.

525: Revolt of Amalafrida against Hilderic crushed at the Battle of Caspa.

526, 30 August: Death of Theodoric, King of the Ostrogoths.

527: Justinian becomes East Roman Emperor.

c.529: The Vandals under Hoamer defeated by Antalas' Moors in Byzacena.

530, 15 June: Gelimer deposes Hilderic.

532: Peace treaty signed between the Romans and Persians.

533: Uprisings of Prudentius in Tripolitania and Godas in Sardinia against Vandal rule. The Romans send troops to support the revolts and Gelimer sends his fleet to Sardinia.

533, summer: Belisarius lands in Africa.

533, 13 September: The Vandals defeated at Ad Decimum.

533, 15 September: The Romans capture Carthage.

533, 15 December: The Vandals defeated at the Battle of Tricamarum.

534: Gelimer captured and sent to Constantinople. Belisarius celebrates a triumph. The Moors raid Byzacena and Numidia.

535: Belisarius made Consul and sails to Sicily to reconquer Italy from the Ostrogoths.

535: Solomon left in charge of Africa. He defeats the Moors at the Battles of Mammes and Mount Bourgaon. He bottles up Iaudas in the Aurès Mountains.

536, spring: Roman troops in Carthage mutiny and appoint Stotzas as their leader. They are joined by the remaining Vandals. Belisarius sails from Sicily to support Solomon. He defeats Stotzas at the Battle of Membresa.

536, winter (or early 537): Germanus defeats Stotzas at the Battle of Scalae Veteres.

539: Solomon defeats Iaudas' Moors at Mount Aurasium.

543: Solomon killed in a skirmish with the Moors. He is succeeded by Sergius, whose misrule rekindles the mutiny and Moorish raids.

545: Stotzas and the last remaining Vandals join the Moors in Byzacena. They defeat the Romans at Sicca Venera. Stotzas is killed in the battle.

545: Gontharius leads another Roman rebellion. Supported by the Vandals, he defeats the Moors at Hadrumentum.

546: Artabanes the Armenian kills Gontharius and Carthage is brought back under Imperial control. The last surviving Vandals are rounded up and sent to Constantinople.

565, November: Death of the Emperor Justinian.

640: The Arabs conquer Egypt.

647: The Arabs invade Roman North Africa.

698: The Arabs capture and destroy Carthage.

The Vandal and Alan Kings

Godegisel (unknown–406). He led the Asding Vandals from central Europe to the Rhine. He died in battle with the Franks on the east bank of the Rhine.

Gunderic (406–428). Son of Godegisel who took over the leadership of the Asdings on his father's death. He led the Asdings through France and into Spain. After their defeat by the Goths in 418, the surviving Silings and Alans came under his rule.

Respendial (dates unknown). Leader of the Alans in 406, who stayed with the Vandals through France and into Spain. He was no longer leading the Alans when they were defeated by the Goths in 418.

Goar (406–c.450). Leader of the group of Alans who broke from Respendial in 406 to join the Romans. He and his followers were given land to settle around Orléans in France.

Sangiban (451). Goar's successor who joined Aetius to defeat the Huns at the Battle of Catalaunian Fields in 451. He and his men fled the field and his fate after the battle is not known.

Addax (unknown–418). Respendial's successor and last king of the independent Alans. He died when the Goths defeated his people and drove the surviving Alans to join up with the Asdings.

Fredibal (unknown–416). The only known leader of the Siling Vandals. He was captured by the Goths and sent to Ravenna as a captive in 416.

Geiseric (428–477). The illegitimate son of Godegisel, born to a concubine. He led the Vandals and Alans into Africa and established the Vandal Kingdom. He had three sons: Huneric, Genzon and Theodoric, as well as a daughter, whose name is not known.

Huneric (477-484). Geiseric's eldest son, who became king on his father's death. Initially married to the daughter of the Visigothic King Theodoric I, he set her aside to marry Eudocia, daughter of Valentinian III, in 455. He had at lest two sons: Hilderic, the eldest, and another whose name is not known. His grandsons, Hoamer and Hoageis, born to his younger son, played a role in the conflicts at the end of the Vandal Kingdom.

Gunthamund (484-496). Son of Genzon and grandson of Geiseric, who became king after his uncle Huneric's death. He had an elder brother, Godagis, who died before 484, leaving Gunthamund as the oldest male of the Asding royal line.

Thrasamund (496-523). Genzon's brother, who married Amalafrida, daughter of King Theodoric of the Ostrogoths. His younger brother, Geilaris, never became king but had three sons; Geilmer, Tzazon and Ammatas, all of whom played leading roles during the Roman reconquest.

Hilderic (523-530). Eldest son of Huneric and Eudocia, who therefore was the grandson of both Geiseric and the Roman Emperor Valentinian III. He let Hoamer, his younger brother's son, lead his armies in battle against the Moors. His pro-Roman policies alienated the Vandal nobles.

Gelimer (530-534). Eldest son of Geilaris, who was the youngest son of Genzon. He usurped the throne from Hilderic and had his uncle executed in 533. Defeated by Belisarius, Gelimer was the last Vandal king. His brothers, Tzazon and Ammatas, commanded Vandal armies which supported Gelimer's stand against Belisarius.

The Later Roman Emperors

Gratian (375-383). Western Emperor overthrown by Magnus Maximus.

Valentinian II (375-392). Proclaimed co-Emperor of the West by the Army of Gaul at the age of four. He rules as a figurehead until his death – either by suicide or murdered by Arbogast, his Frankish Magister Militum.

Theodosius I (379-395). Appointed Eastern Emperor by Gratian, he later extended his control over the whole empire. He established the Nicene version of Christianity as the state religion.

Magnus Maximus (382-388). British usurper defeated by Theodosius.

Eugenius (392-394). Pagan usurper elevated by Arbogast and defeated by Theodosius.

Arcadius (383-408). Initially co-Emperor with his father Theodosius and then sole Emperor of the East from 395.

Honorius (393-423). Initially co-Emperor with his father Theodosius and then sole Emperor of the West from 395.

Constantine III (407-411). Proclaimed Emperor by the British Army, he moved into Gaul to establish control over Britain, Gaul and Spain, leaving Honorius controlling only Italy and Africa. He fought against the Vandals in 407 and was defeated by Honorius' general Constantius in 411.

Constans II (409-411). Constantine III's son who was made co-Emperor.

Priscus Attalus (409 and also 414-415). A usurper who was twice proclaimed Emperor by the Goths and was deposed by Honorius' armies.

Maximus (409-411). A Spanish usurper who rose against Constantine III and fled back to Spain when his army mutinied.

Jovinus (411–413). A usurper who briefly filled the vacuum after Constantine III's overthrow in Gaul.

Sebastianus (412–413). Another western usurper who was appointed co-Emperor by Jovianus.

Theodosius II (408–450). Eastern Emperor and son of Arcadius.

Constantus III (421). Honorius' general and son-in-law of Theodosius I, who was briefly recognised as co-Emperor by Honorius.

Joannes (423–425). Proclaimed Emperor of the West after Honorius' death and supported by Aetius. He was deposed by Theodosius II's army.

Valentinian III (425–455). Son of Constantius III and Honorius' sister, Galla Placidia. He became West Roman Emperor when he was only 6-years-old. Galla Placidia ruled as the power behind the throne before he came of age.

Marcian (450–457). A soldier who married Theodosius II's sister, Pulcheria, and became East Roman Emperor on Theodosius II's death.

Petronius Maximus (455). Assumed the Western throne on Valentinian III's death and was killed by the Roman mob as Geiseric's Vandals sailed to Rome.

Avitus (455–456). A Gallo-Roman aristocrat proclaimed Western Emperor with the backing of the Visigoths and deposed by Ricimer.

Majorian (457–461). Made Western Emperor by Ricimer and then deposed after the failure of his attempt to re-conquer Africa from the Vandals.

Leo I (457–474). A soldier who was made East Roman Emperor by Aspar.

Libius Severus (461–465). Made Western Emperor by Ricimer but not recognised by the East.

Anthemius (467–472). An Eastern senator who became Western Emperor as a result of a deal between Ricimer and Leo. He was deposed by Ricimer.

Olybrius (472). Geiseric's son-in-law, who had married Placidia, the youngest daughter of Valentinian III. He died of unknown causes shortly after his elevation to the Western throne.

Glycerius (473-474). Proclaimed Western Emperor by Ricimer's nephew – the Burgundian Gundobad. Deposed by the armies of the Eastern Empire.

Julius Nepos (474-475). Put on the Western throne by the Eastern Emperor Leo.

Leo II (474). Grandson of Leo I, who may have been poisoned shortly after gaining the Eastern throne.

Zeno (474-491). Leo I's son-in-law. He was deposed by Basilicus in 475 but regained the throne in 476.

Basiliscus (475-476). Commander of the fleet defeated by Geiseric in 468 and another brother-in-law of Leo I. He briefly seized the Eastern throne from Zeno.

Romulus Augustulus (475-467). The last West Roman Emperor, placed on the throne by his father, Orestes, who had been Attila the Hun's secretary. He was deposed by the Italian army under Odoacer.

Anastasius I (491-518). Another of Leo I's son-in-laws who was made Eastern Emperor by the Empress dowager, Ariadne.

Justin (518-527). Commander of Anastasius' bodyguard who was proclaimed Emperor by the army.

Justinian (527-565). Justin's nephew who reconquered Africa from the Vandals.

Glossary

Africa Proconsularis: The Roman province including Carthage which roughly equates to the coastal area around modern Tunis.

Alamanni: A Germanic tribe living on the upper Rhine.

Alans: A nomadic Sarmatian people who originated to the north of the Black Sea. Some of them merged with the Vandals.

Arian: Followers of a version of Christianity initially proposed by Arius, which was preached to the Goths and other Germans by Ulfilas in the fourth century. It held that Jesus was from God but not the same as God the Father. It was declared heretical at the council of Nicaea in 325. I have used the term 'Catholic' to describe those Christians who held the Nicene Creed in contrast to the Arians.

Asdings: A Vandal clan whose leaders emerged to become the royal line.

Auxilia Palatina: A unit of elite infantry capable of mobile operations as well as standing firm in line of battle – probably about 500 men at full strength.

Baccaudae: A name given to native Romans who had broken from Imperial control to run their own affairs. There were endemic *Baccaudae* uprisings throughout the fifth century in France and Spain.

Baetica: The Roman province of southern Spain which approximately equates to modern Andalusia.

Bucellarii: Soldiers forming the personal bodyguards and private armies of late Roman generals. The name comes from *bucellatum*, which was a hard tack biscuit forming part of a soldier's rations. Such troops were maintained by the commander himself rather than by the state.

Burgundians: A Germanic people living on the middle Rhine in the early-fifth century.

Byzacena: The Roman province encompassing the inland regions of modern Tunisia, south of Africa Proconsularis.

Carthaginiensis: The Roman province of south-eastern and central Spain, also including the Balearic Isles.

Chillarch: The title of a Vandal noble who commanded 1,000 men.

Comes (Count): A senior Roman officer who commanded troops of the regional field armies.

Comitatenses: Units of the Roman regional field armies.

Dacia: A Roman province roughly equating to modern Romania.

Dromon: A fast single-decked warship.

Dux (Duke): A senior Roman officer who commanded frontier forces.

Excubitores: An elite East Roman guards unit formed by the Emperor Leo in the later-fifth century.

Foederati (federates): Initially barbarian troops serving in the Roman Army under their own leaders. By the sixth century they were regular units possibly recruited from barbarians, usually Germans.

Franks: A German people living along the lower Rhine who later took over and gave their name to France.

Gallaecia: The Roman province of north western Spain encompassing modern Galicia, northern Portugal, Asturias and Leon.

Gaul: The Roman name for an area including modern France, Belgium and parts of Germany west of the Rhine.

Gruethungi: A Gothic clan.

Goths: The most powerful Germanic people in the third to fifth centuries who established two kingdoms inside the Roman Empire. The Visigoths, descended from the clans who crossed the Danube in 376, settled first in western France and later moved into Spain. The Ostrogoths, who remained beyond the Roman frontiers until the late-fifth century, later established a kingdom in Italy.

Heruls: An east Germanic people, 400 of whom served as mercenaries in Belisarius' army in Africa. Later they joined in Stotzas' mutiny.

Huns: A nomadic people from central Asia whose westward movements sparked off the Germanic migrations. 600 of them served with Belisarius in Africa against the Vandals.

Illyricum (Illyria): The Roman name for the area including modern Croatia and parts of the former Yugoslavia.

Legion (legio): By the fourth century a Roman legion was a unit of around 1,000 men who fought on foot with spears, javelins and swords.

Limes: The Roman frontier

Limitanei: Second-rate Roman troops who manned the frontier garrisons.

Lusitania: The Roman province of western Spain, approximately equating to the southern regions of modern Portugal.

Magister Militum (Master of Soldiers): The most senior Roman military commander below the Emperor.

Magister Equitum (Master of Horse): One rank below the *Magister Militum*, who theoretically commanded the cavalry but in reality led a mixed force. Therefore, the *Magister Equitum intra Gallias* commanded the Gallic field army including both horse and foot.

Magister Peditum (Master of Foot): As above, but theoretically commanding the foot. The *Magister Peditum Intra Italiam* commanded both horse and foot in the Italian field army.

Mauritania: The three most westerly provinces of Roman North Africa, encompassing the Mediterranean littoral of modern Algeria and Morocco. From west to east these were: Mauritania Tingitana, Mauritania Caesariensis and Mauritania Sitifensis. Mauritania Tingitana came under the administrative control of Spain rather than Africa.

Moesia: The Roman provinces south of the upper Danube bordering modern Bulgaria.

Moors: The original inhabitants of North Africa and ancestors of the modern Berbers.

Nicene Creed: The Christian orthodoxy stemming from the Council of Nicaea in 325, which holds that Jesus was both God and man.

Notitia Dignitatum: A list of offices and army units of the later Roman Empire.

Numidia: The province to the west of Carthage which straddles the border of modern Tunisia and Algeria. Its main city was Hippo Regius.

Palatini (Palatine): The most senior units of the late Roman field army.

Pannonia: The Roman name for the region of the middle Danube, before the bend, that includes parts of modern Austria, Hungary and Slovenia.

Przeworsk Culture: The name given by archeologists to the artefacts found in the ancient central European homeland of the Vandals.

Raetia: The Roman province encompassing parts of modern Switzerland, southern Germany and northern Italy.

Riparienses: Roman garrison troops manning the river frontiers.

Tarraconensis: The Roman province of northern Spain.

Tervingi: A Gothic clan who formed the bulk of the army which defeated the Romans at Adrianople in 378.

Tingitana: A Roman province encompassing the Mediterranean coastal regions of modern Morocco – more properly Mauritania Tingitana.

Tripolitania: A Roman province encompassing the coastal regions of modern Libya.

Sarmatians: A nomadic Iranian people who moved into the area beyond the Roman middle Danube frontier in the second century. The Alans were a Sarmatian people.

Silings: A Vandal clan settled in modern Silesia before the migrations. After their defeat by the Goths, the survivors were absorbed by the Asdings.

Suevi: A Germanic people, from modern Swabia, who joined in the Vandal migration and settled in Spain.

Vexillation: A detachment of a larger unit and the name given to cavalry units in the later Roman Army.

Select Bibliography

Primary Sources

Ammianus Marcellinus, *Res Gestae.*
Anonymous, *Gallic Chronicle of 452.*
Anonymous, *Origin of the Lombard People.*
Augustine of Hippo, *Letters.*
Cassius Dio, *Roman History.*
Claudian, *On the Consulship of Stilicho.*
Gregory of Tours, *History of the Franks.*
Hydatius, *Chronicle.*
Isidore of Seville, *History of the Kings of the Goths, Vandals and Suebi.*
Jerome, *Chronicle.*
Jordanes, *Getica.*
Notitia Dignitatum.
Olympiodorus of Thebes, *History.*
Orosius, *History against the Pagans.*
Paul the Deacon, *History of the Lombards.*
Procopius, *History of the Wars.*
Prosper of Aquitaine, *Chronicle.*
Salvian, *De Gubernatione Dei.*
Sidonius Apollinaris, *Poems and Letters.*
Strategikon of Maurice.
Tacitus, *Germania.*
Victor of Vita, *History of the Persecutions in Africa.*
Zacharias of Mytilene, *Chronicle.*
Zosimus, *New History.*

Secondary Sources

The following sources are those I have found most useful in writing this book. I recommend all of them to readers who wish to learn more about the rise and fall of the Vandal Kingdom and its interactions with the late Roman Empire.

Bachrach, Bernard S. *A History of the Alans in the West*, (Minneapolis, 1973).

Boss, Roy. *Justinian's Armies*, (Stockport, 1993).

Bury, J. B. *The Invasion of Europe by the Barbarians*, (London, 1928).

Bishop, Micheal C., and Coulston, Jon C. N. *Roman Military Equipment from the Punic Wars to the Fall of Rome*, (London, 2006).

Courtois, Christian. *Les Vandales et l'Afrique*, (Paris, 1955).

Delbrück, Hans. *The Barbarian Invasions*, Translated by Walter J Renfroe. (Nebraska, 1990).

Drinkwater, J. F. and Elton, H. *Fifth-century Gaul: A Crisis of Identity*, (Cambridge, 1992).

Dixon, K. and Southern, P. *The Roman Cavalry*, (London, 1992).

Elton, Hugh. *Warfare in Roman Europe, AD 350-425*, (Oxford, 1996).

Gibbon, Edward. *The Decline and Fall of the Roman Empire*, (London 1777-88).

Goldsworthy, Adrian. *The Fall of the West*, (London, 2009).

Gordon, Colin Douglas. *The Age of Attila*, (Toronto, 1966).

Halsall, Guy. *Warfare and Society in the Barbarian West, 450-900*, (London, 2003).

— *Barbarian Migrations and the Roman West*, (Cambridge, 2007).

Heather, Peter. *The Fall of the Roman Empire: A New History of Rome*, (Oxford, 2006).

— *The Goths*, (Oxford, 1996).

Hodgkin, Thomas, *The Barbarian Invasions of the Roman Empire Vol II. The Huns and the Vandals*, (London 1892, reprinted 2001).

Hoffmann, Deitrich. *Das Spaetroemische Bewegungsheer und die Notitia Dignitatum*, (Düsseldorf, 1970).

Hughes, Ian. *Stilicho: The Vandal Who Saved Rome*, (Pen and Sword, 2010).

Lot, Ferdinand. *The End of the Ancient World and the Beginning of the Middle Ages*, (Paris, 1939).

Jacobsen, Torsten Cumberland, *A History of the Vandals*, (Pennsylvania, 2012).

Jones, A. H. M. *The Late Roman Empire 284-602*, (Oxford, 1964).

Junkelmann, M. *Die Reiter Roms*, (Mainz, 1993).

Kelly, Christopher. *Attila the Hun. Barbarian Terror and the Fall of the Roman Empire*, (London, 2008).

Kulikowski, Michael. *Late Roman Spain and its Cities*, (Baltimore, 2004).

Lurrwark, E. N. *The Grand Strategy of the Roman Empire*, (London, 1976).

MacDowall, Simon. *Late Roman Infantryman*, (Oxford, 1994).

— *Late Roman Cavalryman*, (Oxford, 1995).

— *Germanic Warrior*, (Oxford, 1996).

— *The Battle of Adrianople*, (Oxford, 2001).

Merrills, Andy H. and Miles, Richard. *The Vandals*, (Oxford, 2010).

Moorhead, John. *Victor of Vita: History of the Vandal Persecution.* Translated, (Liverpool, 1992).

Moss, J. R. '*The Effects of the Policies of Aetius on the History of Western Europe*', *Historia LXXII*, (1973).

Muhlberger, Stephen. *The Fifth-Century Chroniclers: Prosper, Hydatius, and the Gallic Chronicler of 452*, (Cambridge, 1981).

Thompson, Edward, A. *Romans and Barbarians: The Decline of the Western Empire*, (Madison, 1982).

Tredgold, Warren. *Byzantium and its Army, 284–1081*, (Stanford, 1995).

Ueda-Sarson, Luke. *The Notitia Dignitatum*, http://lukeuedasarson.com/NotitiaPatterns.html

Wallace-Hadrill, John M. *The Barbarian West 400–1000*, (Oxford, 1967).

Index